Suicide

*This book is dedicated to Irvin Kupper (1926–2004),
a dedicated professional, a kind and devoted family man,
and the grandfather of Steve's three children, Jordan, Bryan, and Madison.*

Suicide

THEORY, PRACTICE, AND INVESTIGATION

RONALD M. HOLMES
UNIVERSITY OF LOUISVILLE

STEPHEN T. HOLMES
UNIVERSITY OF CENTRAL FLORIDA

SAGE Publications
Thousand Oaks ▪ London ▪ New Delhi

For information:

Sage Publications, Inc.
2455 Teller Road
Thousand Oaks, California 91320
E-mail: order@sagepub.com

Sage Publications Ltd.
1 Oliver's Yard
55 City Road
London EC1Y 1SP
United Kingdom

Sage Publications India Pvt. Ltd.
B-42, Panchsheel Enclave
Post Box 4109
New Delhi 110 017 India

Library of Congress Cataloging-in-Publication Data

Holmes, Ronald M.
Suicide: Theory, practice, and investigation / Ronald M. Holmes, Stephen T. Holmes.
   p. cm.
Includes bibliographical references and index.
ISBN 1-4129-1009-9 (cloth)
ISBN 1-4129-1010-2 (pbk.)
  1. Suicide. 2. Suicide—United States. I. Holmes, Stephen T.
II. Title.
HV6545.H64 2006 2005
362.28—dc22   2005003607

Contents

Preface

Suicide has been an academic interest for me (Ronald Holmes) ever since the first time I picked up Ronald Maris's book *Social Forces in Urban Suicide*. Despite having a great-grandfather who committed suicide a year after my great-grandmother's death, and despite our religion, Roman Catholic, we were always taught that suicide was wrong and particularly a sin against God.

As Steve and I both began our academic careers as college professors, suicide became a topic that we realized deserved serious research. It became a topic for discussion, especially as it related to the subject matter we taught. Steve and I are both interested in the same research, although he tends to be more quantitative than me (where did I go wrong?). But suicide was always a topic on the edge of our discussions and lectures.

In January 2003, I was elected coroner of Louisville, Kentucky. This is the 16th largest jurisdiction in the United States. A coroner in the commonwealth of Kentucky is the highest-ranking law enforcement agent, with special rights not available to traditional law enforcement personnel. The coroner's responsibility is to determine the cause and manner of death. The coroner also may enter a death scene without a search warrant. I am amazed at the authority a coroner has.

When I first started to attend death scenes, be they at the hospital, a home, the scene of a fatal accident, or a homicide on the street, I knew that the world on the streets held for me a far different perspective from that of the classroom. I was psychologically unprepared for the scenes I would see. The deaths of children, the elderly, the youth, and the ill, as well as the accidents, will stay with me as long as I live. But what has captured my interest, and what I find most difficult to understand, is the person who commits suicide.

As I went from one suicide to another, I gained some understanding of the dynamics of suicide, the investigation of suicide, and the impact that suicide has on the survivors. I also thought that in most cases of suicide, notes and letters were left behind. In our experience, in the majority of suicides there are no notes. But the ones that are left contain a great deal of information about the victim's world and the stated reasons for committing suicide.

When Steve and I decided to write this book, we were aware of various texts and articles that existed concerning suicide. Most dealt with the various theories of suicide, the social statistics of suicide, and an examination of the social core variables of suicide. We decided that we were going to write a book that looked at suicide in a much different way. It would not be a purely investigative book, but one that looked at suicide from various perspectives. We would look at theories of suicide, the types of suicide, suicide among various groups, an analysis of the suicide missives left at the death scenes, the investigation of suicide, and a look into the crystal ball about the future of our society and suicide. We believe this perspective is different from that of the other books. We have attempted to look at the latest literature on suicide and, at the same time, look at the practical world. We were able to use the latter perspective because of my position as coroner. Access to case files—while simultaneously protecting the identity of the deceased and the privacy of the survivors—gave us firsthand knowledge of important information, not knowledge gleaned from second- and third-hand sources.

Who do you thank for a book like this? In our other books, the list was easy to assemble. In this book, however, it is very difficult. We cannot thank those who decided that life held no promise and that death was the only solution to their problems. That would be crass and inhumane. We cannot thank the survivors, even though as coroner, I have extended my personal sympathy and a willingness to help them in any way my office could. The criminal justice system, the mental health professionals, the medical personnel, and others in the helping and investigative agencies certainly do what they can, and for that, we are appreciative. There are angels in this world, and maybe in the case of those caught in despair, anguish, pain, suffering, aloneness, and other circumstances where life no longer seems to have meaning, these angels try as best they can to serve while the person is still alive, and attend to those items that will prepare the deceased as well as possible.

RMH

STH

Acknowledgments

The contributions of the following reviewers are gratefully acknowledged.

Martin Urbina, University of Wisconsin–Milwaukee
Department of Criminal Justice, Milwaukee, WI 53201

Tom Petee, Auburn University
Department of Criminal Justice, Auburn, AL 36849

Steve Stack, Wayne State University
Department of Criminal Justice, Detroit, MI 48202

Cliff Bryant, Virginia Tech
Blacksburg, VA 24061

1

Suicide in the United States

Suicide is an ageless concern. It leaves families, intimates, and friends of the victim devastated and often causes a lingering feeling of malaise. Forbidden in the Bible, suicide has nonetheless become such a practical problem that it is now an everyday concern. No society condones or encourages suicide as a wholesale practice. It leaves us with a feeling that we as a society have somehow failed the person who committed suicide, suggesting that we should have known what the person was thinking and taken action to help.

Under certain circumstances, a society might permit suicide. For example, in Japan, up until a few years ago, a person who somehow brought great shame to him- or herself, or to his or her family or society was encouraged to commit suicide as a way to erase that shame. The ritual of disembowelment was performed in front of witnesses. The manner in which the suicide was carried out, the pain that was self-inflicted, was an instrument for the person to remove as much of the shame he or she caused as possible. For example, if the person not only inserted the ritualistic knife into his or her stomach but were able to reach inside his or her body cavity, extend the intestines, and cut them in two, any shame would be removed, thereby guaranteeing everlasting life. This practice is no longer in vogue.

In other cases, a person might deliberately give up his or her life for a cause. Japanese pilots in World War II intentionally dived their planes into Allied ships, hoping many would be killed by their heroic actions.

There are many examples of suicide in history, and in Chapter 2, we will examine suicidal behaviors as they have existed in human history.

> Jack,
>
> Hi, I love you. You have been a great friend this year. I appreciate your desire to help and make me smile again, laugh better. . . . Don't be sad. I am happy and at peace.
>
> Love, Grace
>
> Excerpt from a suicide note, Louisville, KY.

Suicide should never be treated lightly. To tell someone to jump from a bridge just might result in the individual's doing so. The decision to commit suicide is often weighed down by situational stressors, physical demands or strife, or a multitude of other concerns and conflicts that we will never understand completely. Maybe Emile Durkheim was right when he talked of stressors, both internal and external to the personality, as being greatly responsible for the person's decision to commit suicide. That, too, we will examine in another chapter.

This chapter's focus is not on the causes of suicide. Rather, we will examine some of the facts and statistics of suicide. These data are important in order to understand the traits and characteristics of the person who commits suicide, gender differences and marital status of those who commit suicide, as well as other selected social variables. But first, let us examine the general perspective of suicide.

What Is Suicide?

Basic Definitions

Generally speaking, suicide is simple to define. It is the act of killing oneself. Despite this simple definition as "self-murder," no one commits suicide for the same reasons and under the same circumstances. In other words, suicide is a behavior that differs from one person to another and from one time to another and has different motivations and anticipated gains. For example, someone may take his or her life to escape the pain of cancer. In another case, such as the one that occurred recently in Louisville, Kentucky, a 17-year-old boy took his own life by putting a shotgun under his chin. He was upset with his girlfriend because she was talking to another boy after school while he was waiting in his car to take her home. In another recent case investigated by the Louisville coroner's office, a 21-year-old man killed his girlfriend and then himself with the same gun. The reason? She had just taken out a protective warrant against him, and he was infuriated.

As we can see from these three examples, the circumstances were all different. The anticipated gains were also different. In the first instance, the person wanted to escape the pain of cancer. In the second instance, suicide was the choice as a solution to a perceived vital issue. In the third instance, the young man killed out of anger and committed suicide as a further victimization from his ex-girlfriend.

As we have done in several books dealing with serial murder and mass murder, we believe it is helpful to examine the issue of suicide by using certain categories. With serial killers, categories such as *visionary, mission, hedonistic,* and *power/control* were developed to differentiate among the various serial killers we discussed. In mass murder, other types were discussed, such as *family annihilator, disgruntled employee,* and *disgruntled citizen.* With suicide, there is no better typology to use than Durkheim's. In a subsequent chapter, we will discuss *anomic, egoistic,* and *altruistic* suicide types. Then, we will add a fourth—*fatalistic.* But other types exist as well. For example, one theorist offers a *dutiful* type. We will discuss the four major types offered above, but we will also include *dutiful, existential, revengeful,* and *political or ideological* types.

The Extent of Suicide

With approximately 30,000 people a year taking their own lives, suicide results in more deaths than does homicide. Suicide ranks 11th as a leading cause of death in the United States, whereas homicide ranks 14th. In addition, suicide is the third leading cause of death among young people between the ages of 15 and 24.

In looking at the data in Table 1.1, it is apparent that if one examines only the raw numbers, suicides outnumber homicides by more

Table 1.1   Comparison of Suicide and Homicide in the United States, 2000

Year	Suicides	Homicides
2000	29,350	12,943

Note: The latest year available for both sets of data is 2000.

Table 1.2   Suicide by Hours, Days, Weeks, and Months, 2000 (in percentages)

Hour	Day	Week	Month
3.4	80.4	564.4	2,445.8

Note: Total number of suicides in 2000 = 29,350.

than 44%. Let us take a further look at some of the generic data of suicide.

Table 1.2 illustrates the magnitude of the suicide problem in this country. Of course, these numbers alone do not account for the total suffering and loss. For every suicide victim, there are many other people affected. Family members often seem to feel some responsibility for the suicide victim's behavior. They, too, are victims.

When looking at the numbers and rates of suicide victims, some social core variables are involved. One, for example, is age. One may argue from looking at the rates that the older the person, the greater the wish to die. However, there are some exceptions, and Table 1.3 demonstrates this very well.

As one examines the suicide rate according to age, with the exception of ages 35–54, the suicide rate goes up gradually. As one approaches the age cohort of 85+, it is apparent that the older the person, the greater the wish to die. There are some clear reasons for this. First of all, and this is especially true for men, the personal perception of suicide may change gradually. The status of occupation has faded for all practical purposes. Additionally, the person's health is generally fading, and illnesses and diseases are both more likely and more likely to be debilitating. Regardless of the reason(s), generally speaking, the

Table 1.3   Suicide Rates by Age, 2000

Age Cohort	Suicide Rate
5–14	0.08
15–24	10.4
25–34	12.8
35–44	14.6
45–54	14.6
55–64	12.3
65–74	12.6
75–84	17.7
85+	19.4

Source: Vital Statistics of the United States (2000).

older the person the more likely he or she is to consider suicide an option. When we move into the chapter on suicide and the elderly, this issue will become more apparent and noteworthy.

Suicide Attempts

There are about 25 attempts for every completed suicide. As far as gender is concerned, men are more successful at committing suicide than women are. An old axiom often cited is that three times as many men commit suicide than women, but three times as many women attempt suicide without a successful completion than men. This may be true for many reasons. One could be that men are more apt to use a firearm at their disposal than are women. The Bureau of Justice Statistics (2002) reports that men are seven times more likely to use a firearm to take their own lives than are women. It may also be that men are more likely to have some familiarity with firearms than are women. Thus, they are more successful than women in using such a weapon.

Regardless of the reason, the same report stated that women are three times more likely to attempt suicide, and men are three times more successful in completing the suicidal act.

As we can see from the data in Table 1.4, suicide ranks as the 11th leading cause of death in the United States. This total number may not be accurate, and from the experience we have in death investigation, we

Table 1.4   Leading Causes of Death in the United States, 2000

Rank and Cause of Death	Rate	Deaths
1. Heart disease	258.2	710,760
2. Malignant neoplasms	200.9	553,092
3. Cerebrovascular diseases	60.9	167,661
4. Chronic lower respiratory disease	44.3	122,009
5. Accidents	35.6	97,902
6. Diabetes mellitus	25.2	69,301
7. Influenza and pneumonia	23.7	65,313
8. Alzheimer's disease	18.0	49,558
9. Nephritis, nephrosis	13.5	37,251
10. Septicemia	11.3	31,224
11. Suicide	10.7	29,350

Source: National Center for Health Statistics (2002).

are certain it is not. For example, some deaths may be ruled accidental, natural, or homicide in error by one of the components of the criminal justice system. In one case, Ronald Holmes was personally involved in opening a case ruled a homicide but was later determined to be a suicide. On the other hand, another case had been ruled by a deputy coroner as a suicide, but it was clearly a case of an autoerotic fatality. The coroner's office was apparently not as well versed as it should have been in determining what was truly autoerotic behavior and the necessary signs of that behavior to look for at the death scene.

The point is that some suicides are hidden. Therefore, the accuracy of the reported numbers must be taken with some skepticism, and the true number may never be known.

Marital Status and Suicide

There is a strong relationship between suicide and marital status. Single people commit suicide more often than married people (Mastekaasa, 1995; Pasewark & Fleer, 1993). Widowed people kill themselves more often than married people do but less often than single people do. Luoma and Pearson (2002) reported that 1 in 400 white American widowed males in the age cohort of 20–34 will die by suicide in any given year. That number is compared to 1 in 9,000 married men in the general population. To reinforce this point, Pearson (1998) reported that white men, aged 25–34, were 17 times more likely to kill themselves and black men in that same age cohort were nine times more likely to kill themselves than the general population.

Thus, there appears to be a direct relationship between marital status and the will to live. This seems to be especially true when one examines young widowed people, single adults, and elderly widowed males.

Occupation and Suicide

Frequently, we are told that certain occupations—dentists, police officers, psychologists, laborers, prison guards—have the greatest risk for suicide. These reports become almost urban legends.

In particular, policing is a stressful and often debilitating occupation. The stress of everyday interaction with law enforcement issues may contribute to a high rate of suicide. For example, Hackett (2003) reported that more police officers kill themselves every year than are killed by felons or die in other duty-related activities. Many departments have developed programs and offices to deal with the problem of suicide among their officers. Both Loo (2003) and Hackett (2003) call for departments to develop a "postvention" program, a strategy that will combat police who may try to commit suicide through early identification of personality types, a standard operating procedure for intervention, a crisis team to perform the intervention, and a debriefing episode.

Physicians also have a high rate of suicide, perhaps because of the stress involved in the practice of medicine. The high stress of dealing with patients who are ill and many times terminally ill may take a terrible toll on the psychological health of physicians. Additionally, treating physicians who are experiencing suicidal ideation poses unique problems. As Schneck (1998) pointed out, physicians who are ill may have problems with role reversal and the "VIP" syndrome.

They do not become the best of patients or respond to treatment favorably.

Suicide experts now inform us that there is no significant statistical relationship between suicide and occupation (Foxhall, 2001). Even if one occupation is more prone statistically to commit suicide, the occupation itself does not explain the reason for the suicide rate.

Other problems may exist in the collection of information concerning occupation and suicide. For example, on the death certificate (see Figure 1.1), there is a section that seeks the "Decedent's Usual Occupation." We have noted in our research on death certificates that many times, the occupation is not listed or is "unknown." This practice has changed in recent years, but if this lack of completion is prevalent in other U.S. coroners' offices, then one can easily see that how integral or irrelevant occupation is as a predictor of suicide is missing, and thus lacking in import in suicide research.

Regional Differences and Suicide

Rates of suicide vary from one region of the country to the next. The Centers for Disease Control and Prevention in Atlanta gather data concerning rates of suicide in four regions: Northeast, Midwest, South, and West. Table 1.5 lists the regions and their rate of suicide per 100,000 people.

Contrary to what some may believe, the suicide rate in the Northeast region is actually the lowest in the country, with a rate of 8.6 suicides per 100,000 people. Vermont and Maine have the highest rates within the region, whereas New Jersey and New York have the lowest rates.

In the Midwest region, the overall suicide rate is 10.9 per 100,000 people. The states are all fairly close around the mean. For example, the lowest suicide rate exists within Illinois and the highest is in South Dakota.

The West has the next highest rate of suicide, with a overall rate of 11.8 per 100,000 people. The states with the highest rates are Wyoming, Montana, and Arizona. Pasewark and Fleer (1993) addressed the relatively high rate of suicide in Wyoming by stressing that it may be accounted for by accessibility of lethal weapons, the lack of social

MUST BE TYPED	1. DECEDENT'S NAME (First, Middle, Last)					2. SEX	3. DATE OF DEATH (Month, Day, Year)	

	4. SOCIAL SECURITY NO.	5a. AGE Last Birthday (Years)	5b. UNDER 1 YEAR		5c. UNDER 1 DAY		6. DATE OF BIRTH (Month, Day, Year)	7. BIRTHPLACE (City/State or Foreign Country)
DECEDENT			(Months)	(Days)	(Hours)	(Minutes)		

8. WAS DECEDENT EVER IN U.S. ARMED FORCES?	9a. PLACE OF DEATH (Check only one)		
		HOSPITAL	OTHER
☐ Yes ☐ No	☐ Inpatient ☐ ER/Outpatient ☐ DOA		☐ Nursing Home ☐ Residence ☐ Other (Specify)

9b. FACILITY NAME (If not institution, give street and number)	9c. CITY, TOWN, OR LOCATION OF DEATH	9d. COUNTY OF DEATH

10. MARITAL STATUS Married, Never Married Widowed, Divorced (Specify)	11. SURVIVING SPOUSE (If wife, give maiden name)	12a. DECEDENT'S USUAL OCCUPATION (Give kind of work done during most of working life. Do Not use retired)	12b. KIND OF BUSINESS/INDUSTRY

13a. RESIDENCE - State	13b. COUNTY	13c. CITY, TOWN, OR LOCATION	13d. STREET AND NUMBER

13e. INSIDE CITY LIMITS?	13f. ZIP CODE	14. WAS DECEDENT OF HISPANIC ORIGIN? (Specify No or Yes – If yes specify Cuban, Mexican, Puerto Rican, etc.)	15. RACE – American Indian, Black, White, etc. (Specify)	16. DECEDENT'S EDUCATION (Specify only highest grade completed)	
				Elem/Secondary (0–12)	College (1–4 or 5+)
☐ Yes ☐ No		☐ No ☐ Yes			

PARENTS

17. FATHER'S NAME (First, Middle, Last)	18. MOTHER'S NAME (First, Middle, Maiden Surname)

19a. INFORMANT'S NAME	19b. MAILING ADDRESS (Street and Number or Rural Route Number, City or Town, State, Zip Code)

INFORMANT

20a. METHOD OF DISPOSITION	20b. PLACE OF DISPOSITION (Name of cemetery, crematory, or other place)	20c. LOCATION (City, Town, or State)
☐ Burial ☐ Cremation ☐ Removal from State ☐ Donation ☐ Other (Specify) _____		

DISPOSITION

21. SIGNATURE OF FUNERAL SERVICE LICENSEE (Or person acting as such)	22. NAME AND ADDRESS OF FACILITY

23a. To the best of my knowledge, death occurred at the time, date, place and due to the causes stated	23b. DATE SIGNED (Month, Day, Year)
CERTIFIER Signature and Title _____ (MUST USE BLACK INK)	

24. NAME AND ADDRESS OF PERSON WHO COMPLETED CAUSE OF DEATH (ITEM 28)

25. TIME OF DEATH	26. DATE PRONOUNCED DEAD (Month, Day, Year)	27. WAS CASE REFERRED TO MEDICAL EXAMINER/CORONER? ☐ Yes ☐ No

28. PART I. Enter the diseases, injuries, or complications that caused death. Do not enter the mode of dying, such as cardiac or respiratory arrest, shock or heart failure. List only one cause on each line. | Approximate interval between onset and death.

IMMEDIATE CAUSE (Final disease or condition resulting in death)	a. _____
	DUE TO (OR AS A CONSEQUENCE OF):
Sequentially list conditions, if any, leading to immediate cause. Enter UNDERLYING CAUSE (Disease or injury that initiated events resulting in death) LAST	b. _____
	DUE TO (OR AS A CONSEQUENCE OF):
	c. _____
	DUE TO (OR AS A CONSEQUENCE OF):
	d.

CAUSE OF DEATH

PART II. Other significant conditions contributed to death but not resulting in the underlying cause given in Part I.	28a. If female, was there a pregnancy in the past 12 months? ☐ Yes ☐ No	28b. Was an autopsy performed? ☐ Yes ☐ No	28c. Were autopsy findings available prior or completion of cause of death? ☐ Yes ☐ No

28d. Did the deceased have Diabetes? ☐ Yes ☐ No	28e. Was Diabetes an immediate, underlying, or contributing cause of or condition leading to death? ☐ Yes ☐ No

29. MANNER OF DEATH	30a. DATE OF INJURY (Month, Day, Year)	30b. TIME OF INJURY	30c. INJURY AT WORK? ☐ Yes ☐ No	30d. DESCRIBE HOW INJURY OCCURRED
☐ Natural ☐ Pending Investigation ☐ Accident ☐ Could not be ☐ Suicide determined ☐ Homicide	30e. PLACE OF INJURY – At home, farm, street, factory, office building, etc. (Specify)		30f. LOCATION (Street and Number or Rural Route Number, City or Town)	

31. REGISTRAR'S SIGNATURE	32. DATE FILED (Month, Day, Year)

REGISTRAR

Figure 1.1   Commonwealth of Kentucky Death Certificate

Table 1.5   Regions and Suicide Rates

Region	Suicide Rate per 100,000 People
Northeast	8.6
Midwest	10.9
South	13.1
West	11.8

Source: Centers for Disease Control and Prevention (2003).

services, and the typical lifestyle in this state. They also said that the availability of weapons, combined with no clear distinctions among males and females using such lethal weapons, greatly influences the rate of suicide by this method. Regardless, we see that Montana has a similar lifestyle, which could account for its high rate. Arizona, however, has a high number of retirement residents; that, combined with many of the same lifestyle components as the other two states, results in its high suicide rate.

The South has the highest suicide rate. Florida and Texas have the highest suicide rates in this region, whereas the District of Columbia has the lowest. Florida has a high rate probably because of its large population of elderly people, and we have already seen the relationship between suicide and age in an earlier section. Why Texas? It may be because of the easy availability of fatal weapons.

Correctional Inmates

Suicide in a correctional institution is a major concern for correctional professionals. Whether because of the manner of incarceration, the lack of a free existence, personal shame, or some other reason, many prisoners commit suicide, and consideration and planning are needed to combat this very real social and human concern.

Who commits suicide in a correctional facility? Serin, Motiuk, and Wichman (2002) reported their findings on males and females in correctional facilities. They broke their sample into two groups: the attempters and the completers. Both groups contained males and females.

Concerning the attempters, Serin et al. found the following:

Males

✓ Single
✓ White
✓ More likely to have committed homicide and breaking and entering, and less likely to have committed sex crimes
✓ In a maximum security institution
✓ Displayed behavioral and emotional problems
✓ Had extensive psychiatric problems
✓ Came from dysfunctional families

Females

✓ Prevalent self-harm behavior
✓ Significant problems with unemployment
✓ Undereducated
✓ Marital/family abuse in many forms (e.g., physical, emotional, sexual, and verbal)
✓ Conflicted community functioning
✓ Grave psychiatric problems
✓ Greatly lacking in cognitive skills

Those who completed suicide had additional traits. For example, the completers were more likely to hang or suffocate themselves, whereas the attempters were more likely to try overdosing or slashing themselves. Additionally, the completers were more likely to be slightly older.

Daigle, Alarie, and Lefebvre (1999) reported that individuals who are in correctional facilities are already in a high suicide risk group for reasons that may include lifestyle and a propensity for risk taking, including several suicide attempts prior to their incarceration. Conner, Duberstein, Conwell, and Caine (2003) reported that merely entering a correctional facility may have gross trauma implications for an inmate. The incarceration experience itself may serve as a final trigger, culminating in the inmate's suicide. The corrections enterprise needs to be aware of such possibilities and extend services, both custodial and therapeutic, to those people who may have been identified as potential suicidal risks.

These findings are important to consider when operating or working in a correctional facility. Interdiction efforts, identification of those who have suicidal ideations, and other important considerations could be strategies for a successful treatment program when examining suicidal behavior in a correctional facility. Thus, staff training becomes an integral part of dealing with the inmate population as well as early identification of predictors of suicidal propensities (Borrill et al., 2003; Lloyd, 1992).

Suicide and the Survivors

With almost every suicide, there are survivors—maybe a spouse, partner, sibling, or child. These survivors are often bereaved by the loss of their loved one and typically have mixed feelings about the suicide.

Feelings usually run the gamut, from loss, anxiety, a feeling of betrayal that the victim did not share feelings with the survivors, shock, disbelief, sadness, and guilt. For many, there is a feeling of self-blame. The survivor may ask what could have been done to prevent the suicide. On the other hand, there may be a stigma attached to survivors. Others may believe the suicide could have been prevented if someone had paid more attention to the pain and suffering the victim experienced. This perceived stigma may prevent some survivors from seeking help.

Of course, the relationship between the person who commits suicide and the survivor certainly has some impact on the survivor's reactions. For example, if an elderly spouse is a survivor, this person may feel some relief if his or her partner was ill or somehow incapacitated. Other sets of relationships may have different reactions. For example, if a young person commits suicide, his or her parents typically question their own parental skills and what they should have done to better help their child.

The children of those who commit suicide are at a higher risk of suicide than are children whose parents do not commit suicide. Although not a child at the time of his death, Ernest Hemingway (who committed suicide) lost his father, his brother, and his sister to suicide. Pulitzer Prize-winning author J. Anthony Lukas's mother also committed suicide.

Of course, survivors are not just family or relatives. Coworkers, for example, are often affected by a suicide. Coworkers have the same questions as family members; Should I have spotted the warning signs? Should I have been more alert to the behavior, the depression, the words and messages? If anyone says words to the effect that "my family would be better off without me" or "I wish I were dead," immediate attention is necessary.

Suicide is a complex behavior. There is no one simple reason, and survivors experience many reactions. Survivors are often forgotten after a suicide, but organizations do exist to help them cope, just as organizations exist to help those who are contemplating suicide. These organizations, such as Survivors of Suicide, preach the message that survivors need help, too. They simply do not get over the death of a loved one. They need care, sympathy, and understanding. They will live on, and they deserve a life without feelings of blame. Group therapy, peer group counseling, or other forms of help should be extended so that the survivor is not another victim.

Conclusion

Suicide must be seen as a societal and personal problem. As a coroner, Ron Holmes has been to many death scenes where the person committed suicide. In one recent case, a husband and wife were having a domestic argument. The husband, an alcoholic, said that if the wife continued harassing him, he would kill himself. She went into the bedroom, took the family gun out of the drawer in a bedstand, walked back into the kitchen, placed it down on the kitchen table, and then told him, in so many words, "Here's the gun, go do it." He picked up the gun and went into the back yard, put the gun under his chin, and pulled the trigger.

When Holmes arrived at the scene, the wife was completely distraught. She told him that her husband had threatened to commit suicide several times before, and she never thought he was serious. She now believed she was in some way responsible for his actions.

·   The motivation for suicide is multifaceted, not understood by the family and other survivors, and certainly not understood by the victim. In Chapter 7, we will look at suicide notes and how convoluted and complex they are. This may be one of the best ways to get into the mind of someone who believes that suicide is *the* solution to a problem.

2

History and Suicide

The wise man will live as long as he ought, not as long as he can.

Seneca

Suicide has been present as long as humankind has existed. Maybe there are no drawings on the walls of caves that depict suicides, as there are of homicides and the killing of animals; nonetheless, as long as events have been chronicled, there have been stories of suicide.

The word *suicide,* however, is relatively new. Broken down into parts, *sui* means "of oneself." *Cide* is derived from the Latin verb *caedere,* which means to cut, chop, or kill. When we translate the Latin, it means literally to "kill oneself." Only a human can commit suicide, just as only a human can commit murder. Suicide is restricted to human beings and must be seen as an intentional act that is sometimes accompanied by gross circumstantial events that "legitimize" the action.

How can that be? If we look at suicide as an act done by a person for whatever reason and for whatever benefit, suicide takes two forms. The first form is individual suicide, in which a person takes his or her life for personal reasons. The reasons may stem from social, health-related, mental, or other seemingly inescapable situations, and the person believes that the only way to solve the problem is suicide (see Figure 2.1). In Chapter 3, we will discuss several types of suicide, examining social integration and societal regulations.

Figure 2.1   A suicide note by the deceased. She discovered that her partner had committed acts of infidelity. The victim was a lesbian, and her lover had contested the coroner's determination of suicide. Her lover stated that the victim was upset but would never have taken her own life. The facts of the case did not support this contention.

The second form of suicide is institutional suicide. In this form, we see that the person is almost "commanded" to commit suicide because his or her life, station, or behavior demands such an action. For example, in ancient Rome, if a general lost a battle or brought some type of shame upon his country, his family, or himself, the only way to remove this stigma was to commit suicide. Later in this book, we will discuss this in more detail. In ancient Japan, ritual disembowelment was the practice if a man brought shame to himself, his family, or his country. The act was to be done not only for the express purpose of removing the shame, but also with rational thought, after great and detailed preparation, and in public. This is obviously quite different from suicide today, with the many pejorative issues and judgments attached.

History has a tale to share with us regarding the extent and the practice of suicide. It is a long history and has been judged differently not only from one society to the next but also by the social class or social standing of the person who commits suicide. For example, in ancient Rome, a serf could hang himself from a tree, but if a general in Caesar's army committed suicide, he certainly would not hang himself. He would use his own sword to end his life. His body then would be treated much differently from the serf's. The act of suicide is the same; the social standing of the two victims is what sets them apart.

Let us move now into a historical analysis of suicide. Societies have viewed and evaluated suicide differently as times have changed, with religion playing a major role each time.

Selected Historical Analysis of Suicide

Suicide in Ancient Greece

Suicide was condemned universally in ancient Greece. Because of the polytheistic belief system that the gods had created humans in service to the gods, humans owed their gods special homage. The goal of the human being, then, was to serve the gods, and committing suicide circumvented this special obligation. In effect, a person would be turning his or her back on the gods and not extending the homage the gods deserve. The person who committed suicide would be seen as a rebel against the gods. The gods would be angry at this act and perhaps not only punish the offender but also wreak havoc on the society that permitted such actions. These ideas were a part of the Greek culture several hundred years before the time of Christ.

Pythagoras, the Greek mathematician, is probably better known for his mathematical formulas, but he had some interesting thoughts about suicide as well. He believed that the world was able to hold only so many souls at one time. Natural order controlled this delicate balance. If people committed suicide—in effect, upsetting the balance of the number of souls—then the whole universe would be in jeopardy.

Plato also had interesting thoughts about suicide. He considered suicide to be an affront to Greek society. Of course, he also believed in some of the religious aspects of the suicide prohibition, but he thought that a man was a soldier of his country, and to commit suicide was akin to desertion from the Greek military. His belief was so strong that he said a man who commits suicide should be buried with no honors or ceremony. Moreover, the person should not have a monument to honor his existence on this earth. To show his human side, Plato also offered that in some circumstances, such as when someone was in extreme pain from an incurable and eventually fatal illness, suicide might be permitted, but that this situation was rare. Usually, someone who committed suicide was burned and placed outside the town limits, and certainly buried away from others who died a more honorable death.

In the next century, Aristotle also condemned suicide. He believed and taught that suicide was an affront against Greek society. Man was a servant of the state and country, and to commit suicide was a personal injury to the country. To take one's own life was a criminal act by the person against the country. As such, that person's personal property was forfeited to the state, and the person was disposed of with no ceremony or dignity.

This is not to say that suicide was *never* permitted. Obviously, in some circumstances, suicide was not only permitted (as in the case for Plato when a person was in unbearable pain) but also encouraged if the person gave up his life in defense of his country. Kodias, for example, was considered a hero when he forfeited his own life in the defense of Athens from the Lacedaemonians. We do the same today. With the September 11, 2001, attack on the United States by terrorists, one side calls the terrorists spineless and despicable men, whereas others call them heroes. What was promised to the men in the planes that attacked the World Trade Center and the Pentagon? Everlasting salvation with all cares and needs satisfied? What was promised to the early church martyrs in the Coliseum in Rome when the lions and the Roman soldiers attacked them? Most likely they were promised everlasting salvation and eternal reward.

Ancient Roman Society and Suicide

Roman society before the time of Christ developed a strong system of dealing with the social issue of suicide. Succinctly put, the

Roman Empire condoned suicide only in certain circumstances and with certain motivations.

In battle, after Rome defeated an enemy, Julius Caesar paraded the heads of his enemies, who chose suicide rather than a fight to the death, through the streets of Rome, demeaning their "cowardly" acts of suicide (White, 1912). But those in the military often committed suicide when defeat seemed inevitable. Leaders of the military who committed suicide with dignity and respect for the Roman establishment were allowed honorable burials within the city instead of dishonorable burials outside of the city. If a soldier's fate was execution by the victors, suicide was the preferred alternative. This brought no dishonor to the person or the family, and the family was still entitled to a full inheritance. In other, related cases, soldiers killed each other rather than be taken captive by the enemy (Fyfe, 1997; Graves, 1996).

In Roman society, suicide was permitted in the aristocracy more than in the lower classes. With the former, suicide was viewed as the freedom to choose for oneself one's own destiny and fate. For the latter, life was a form of slavery, and death brought freedom from the bondage of life.

This does not mean that society necessarily encouraged suicide or that everyone accepted suicide as a viable alternative to life. Certainly, if they knew a person's intentions, most friends and relatives tried to talk that person out of committing suicide.

Methods of suicide also differed by social status. For example, slaves and the lower classes usually committed suicide by hanging or drowning. The upper classes, including the political leaders and the military, typically committed suicide by poison (the former) and their own weapons (the latter).

Suicide was also allowed for members of the aristocracy who were in unbearable pain. For example, one elder committed suicide because of extreme pain from ulcers on his genitals (Graves, 1996). In another case, an older wealthy and influential Roman citizen suffered from such pain that he chose death (Radice, 1963). Atticus, a friend of Cicero, starved himself to death because of the pain from his cancer (Nepos, 1971).

Roman society also allowed suicide as a way to demonstrate loyalty. Wives, soldiers, slaves, and others often committed suicide as a final act of devotion and love. One of the best known cases is that of Mark Antony and his servant, Eros, who used Antony's sword to kill himself despite Antony's plea to kill him. Later, Antony committed suicide. Seneca's wife, Paulina, also committed suicide after the death of her husband. This was not only accepted but lauded, and their bodies were allowed proper burials.

In summary, Rome allowed suicide in certain circumstances when it was done for the honor and glory of Rome or within the prescribed realm of honor. It was considered an honorable end to a life dedicated to the Roman family and country, and was usually reserved for the upper classes and the military. It could erase shame for a personal or professional act, and it enabled a person to escape unbearable pain and suffering.

The gods of Rome were not especially opposed to suicide, and Roman citizens did not consider suicide an affront to the gods, as did the Greeks. If done with rational deliberation and with the proper motivation and methodology, suicide was seen as a positive act, especially for those with social status.

Christianity and Suicide

As Christians gained control over Rome and much of the Western world, attitudes toward suicide changed drastically. Even in the case of Judas, the more important sin in Christianity was the rejection of God's acceptance of any wrong where forgiveness was a possibility. What the person was actually doing was turning his or her back on God, which was judged more seriously than suicide.

Christians shortly after the time of Christ lived a life of asceticism. The afterlife was more important, where one would live in harmony with God and in perfect happiness. The pains and sufferings of this life were inconsequential because of what lay in store in the next life. Many suicides occurred during this time, and Christians went willingly to their deaths at the hands of the Romans because of their belief in life everlasting.

Not until much later—as late as the 4th century—was suicide actually banned by the church (Rev. William Griner, personal interview, September 23, 2003). At that time, church fathers decided that suicide was not only not allowed, it was a sin because the person who committed suicide had, in effect, turned away from God.

During the 5th century, St. Augustine decided that life was a gift from God, and to take one's own life was a rejection of that gift and thus a rejection of God. Augustine and others believed that it was very important to adhere to the Fifth Commandment, "Thou shalt not kill." This referred not only to killing others but also to suicide. It did not matter if the person was in terrible physical or mental agony. Pain was meant to be endured; it was a test of that person and his or her love of God. To take one's life under this circumstance meant not only the person's rejection of God but also a rejection of God's control over life and death. Only God can decide when a person is to die, not man. Suicide became the worst sin, and the person who committed suicide became the worst kind of sinner, damned to spend the rest of eternity in the fires of hell.

Over the next several hundred years, the Church held synods to discuss the status of suicide and the penalties for such a sin. For example, the Synod at Aries in AD 452 prohibited suicide because it was an act of murder. The Synod of Braga in AD 563 declared that in ordinary cases of suicide, the rites of the church would not be extended to the deceased. The Synod of Toledo in AD 693 stated that anyone who committed suicide would be excommunicated from the church and thus not eligible for last rites or burial in consecrated ground. This last declaration was reinforced at the Synod at Nimes in AD 1096, when the church leaders forbade those who committed suicide to be buried in "white soil" and required their burial outside the churchyard and, in some cases, outside the city. Customs followed later that demanded that the body of one who had committed suicide be dragged through the streets and a stake driven into it. In another custom, the body of a person who had committed suicide could not be removed from the house through the door; early church fathers decreed that this was reserved for those who lived free of sin. Instead, the body had to be removed through a window. If the window was too small, a larger hole would have to be made.

Later, church leaders reinforced the attitudes and practices of the early Christians. For example, in the 13th century, St. Thomas Aquinas declared that suicide was an unnatural act, an act against society, and because life was a gift from God, it was a rejection of God.

Suicide in the Bible

The Bible contains several examples of suicide. Perhaps the most famous is that of Judas. Judas, an apostle of Christ, betrayed Him for 30 pieces of silver. As Matthew 27:3–5 says, "Then Judas, which had betrayed Him, when he saw that he was condemned, repented himself, and brought again the thirty pieces of silver to the chief priest and elders, saying, 'I have sinned against innocent blood.' And they said, 'What is that to us? See thou to that.' And he cast down the pieces of silver in the temple, and departed and went out and hanged himself." Some would argue that Judas's worst sin was not the act of suicide, but that he did not believe in the possibility of forgiveness from God.

In the Old Testament, there is a story of Ahithopel, a counselor to King David. Leaving David's camp, Ahithopel joined another's, but changed his mind later and killed himself (II Samuel 17:23). King Saul, the first king of Israel, felt abandoned by God. He sought the services of witches, but that, too, failed. He finally fell upon his own sword because he was losing a battle with enemies, and rather than face the shame of defeat, he committed suicide. Another king, King Zimri, was defeated in battle after being king only seven days; he could not face the shame of defeat and set his house on fire while he was inside it (I Kings 16:18–19).

Certainly, the Old Testament holds a message for those who commit suicide. How much it influenced the thoughts and dogma of the Christians in the early years after the time of Christ, and even up to the present, is immeasurable. It is safe to say that suicide is still seen by many as a sin, and the only "reward" for it is believed to be eternal suffering in the afterlife.

What do many contemporary religions say about suicide today? Obviously, the Catholic Church is officially opposed to anyone's committing suicide. Life is a precious gift from God, and suicide goes against one of humankind's most important ideals: the preservation of life. To discard that gift is the utmost tragedy. Of course, as occurred in the Middle Ages, if one were faced with the possibility of having one's virginity violated or offering one's life in the face of martyrdom, then suicide would be looked at differently, in a more positive way. The *Catholic Encyclopedia* goes even further. This publication "considers that those unfortunates . . . who attempt to take their life often act through malice or culpable cowardice" (p. 342). But many people believe that those who resort to suicide are experiencing some type of pain—psychological, physical, or other—and the only way to remove themselves from this pain is to end their lives.

In many of the Protestant faiths, the official position of that church will depend on the minister. For example, in several of the Baptist churches we have interviewed, if the minister preaches an accepting philosophy of suicide, then the church members in turn are more accepting of it. Conversely, if the minister is dogmatically opposed, then the church members will often follow that teaching. We have also found this to be true of other Protestant faiths. Presbyterians, for example, have an official position of unacceptance, but it will also depend upon the person's personal circumstances at the time of the suicide. Thus, it appears that the members of a church will mirror the teaching of their minister. If they are opposed to the teaching at the time, they will move to another church that is in more congruence with their own beliefs.

The Buddhist religion, on the other hand, contains rules that Buddhists cannot commit suicide, and if one does, that person has grievously sinned. People are prohibited from committing suicide because they are encouraged to make constructive use of their life and make good choices so that the future can be changed for the better (Florida, 1993).

Within the Islamic faith, committing suicide is a grave sin. Many view a person who has committed suicide as someone who has turned his or her back on Islam. The faithful can pray to Allah to forgive someone who commits suicide. So, it is permitted to mention a person who has committed suicide and pray to Allah to forgive that person.

Case History

A 29-year-old woman had tried to take her own life several times in the past year. Two weeks before her final, and successful, attempt, she went into her garage and closed all the doors and windows. She tried to start her car but was unsuccessful. Her family learned of the latest attempt and had her hospitalized in a local medical facility. Only 2 days after her release, she went back into her garage again, arranged a tarp on the concrete floor, and shot herself one time in the side of her head.

This woman left no suicide note. Her psychiatrist told the local coroner that she was very upset with life itself. Confessing to drug problems, a lack of focus in her life, family problems, and other issues that confused and confounded her, she decided to end her own life. The reason? To find peace.

With compassion for her case, her priest buried her in the local Catholic cemetery. What would have been her final religious ministrations less than 200 years ago? Certainly much different.

Emerging Ideas on Suicide

It was not until the 18th and the early part of the 19th centuries that suicide was seen as something that could be explained in part through the medical model. Suicide was now not an act in rebellion against God, not a sin, but rather an act by someone with a serious mental condition.

The belief emerged that a person's decision to commit suicide should rest with that person. If physical pain was too unbearable, or if life was too painful, a person had the right to decide on suicide. Suicide was seen as not wrong in itself, just that it prohibits the person from doing any more social good. Coupling that thought with the medical model, no person would commit suicide if that person's life was fulfilling and enjoyable.

In the late 19th and the 20th centuries, attitudes toward suicide changed again. For example, Schopenhauer (1788–1860) believed that suicide was a prerogative for the individual. Life was misery, and a person did not commit suicide because he did not want to live, but because he was not happy with the conditions of life around him. Kant

(1724–1804), on the other hand, believed that suicide was never acceptable. Nietzsche (1844–1900) believed in the right to suicide.

The medical field slowly entered the thinking on suicide. Psychiatry, for example, was not an acceptable practice until the beginning of the 19th century, when it began to grow in prominence and influence. People began to believe that the person who committed suicide had to be mentally ill. Durkheim (1858–1917) gave us a different perspective. Speaking on the role of society and its influence on human behavior, he wrote his book on suicide wherein he developed four types of suicide: egoistic, fatalistic, altruistic, and anomic. This typology is still used today. Durkheim's contribution to our understanding of suicide is the relationship between society and the person who commits suicide. We will explore these relationships in the next chapter.

In the 20th century, the medical model grew dramatically in importance. Depression came to be seen the main reason for suicide. Existential philosophy, as espoused by Sartre (1905–1980), denied such claims offered by the medical model and supported the belief that anyone who commits suicide possesses absolute free will, thus carrying the responsibility for his or her life and death. Camus (1913–1960) believed that suicide was not a solution to life's problems. He felt that life was worth living and should be lived as long as possible.

Overall, though, regardless of various beliefs (those of philosophers, psychologists, psychiatrists, and social and other behavioral scientists), suicide was still viewed in a negative light. The victim's family felt shame because others believed they somehow failed the deceased and could have done more to prevent the death.

Conclusion

As we have seen in this chapter, suicide has been viewed differently over time and in different societies. The influence of the Greeks and Romans has faded as we moved into the 21st century, but many people still believe that suicide is a "cowardly" act committed by someone who has turned from God and rejected the "blessings of pain and sorrow."

Perhaps we are looking at the issue of suicide differently now and accepting more the teachings of psychology and psychiatry about the mental aspects of those who commit suicide. Some would call us more enlightened, whereas others pray for our souls but neglect the souls of those who deserve their prayers more.

3

Theories and Types of Suicide

Social and behavioral scientists have developed typologies to explain various forms of human behavior. But with regard to suicide, few typologies, if any, are better known or more valuable for analysis than that developed by Emile Durkheim.

Emile Durkheim

Emile Durkheim was born in 1858. His father was a rabbi in his hometown of Lorraine, France, and his mother, Melanie, was a home-maker. He was educated at the College of d'Epinal and the Ecole Normale Superieure, and was later admitted a teacher of philosophy but taught many courses in sociology, topics including crime, law, and religion (Simpson, 1963; Thompson, 1982).

Durkheim's published works include *The Division of Labor in Society; Ethics and the Sociology of Morals; Sociology and Philosophy;* and, for our purposes, his most important, *Suicide: A Study in Sociology.* More sociology than philosophy, Durkheim's works influenced many social scientists into the 20th century, especially in the area of suicide. Durkheim died at the age of 59 in 1917.

Durkheim's work is so valuable because he examined suicide from social and societal perspectives rather than a religious or psychological one. Using the scientific method of the times, Durkheim saw suicide as a phenomenon that arose from societal pressures and influences.

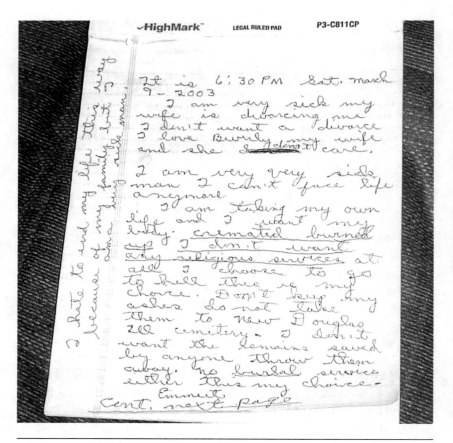

Figure 3.1   A suicide note left by a 35-year-old man. From the note, he admits his life is not what he thinks it should be. He admits to being ill, and his wife has left him. He also leaves some last wishes.

Source: Courtesy of the Jefferson County (Kentucky) Coroner's Office.

Durkheim's Suicide Typology

Durkheim viewed suicide as a social act, not as a sin or a transgression against society. His point of view was certainly radically different from that of the church of the Middle Ages, and he was at constant variance with religious groups. By this time, other societies had also started to rethink their positions about those who commit suicide. It was truly time for a new perspective.

> *Integration*—the extent of social relations binding a person or a group to others, such that they are exposed to the moral demands of the group.
>
> *Regulation*—the normative or moral demands placed on the individual that come with membership in a group.
>
> *Source:* Bearman (1992), p. 503.

Durkheim realized that within every citizen existed two dimensions: integration and regulation. Integration is the manner in which the individual assimilates into the society, how much one becomes a part of the society and culture. This is very important in order for a person to exist in harmony with society. On the other hand, there is also social regulation, which is how the person acknowledges and abides by society's rules.

How a person adapts to the demands of society and accepts the regulations of the group will, in some measure, account for how well he or she fits into society and accepts his or her station and circumstances. Durkheim argued that the ways in which the two dimensions are arranged and rearranged will influence behavior, and when the two dimensions are either too strong or too weak, they may account for the suicidal personality.

Durkheim categorized four types of suicide: anomic, altruistic, egoistic, and fatalistic. Table 3.1 illustrates these four types and the manner in which integration and regulation influence each type of suicide. Note that Durkheim's categorization ignored the psychological or psychiatric elements that may be responsible for suicide.

Table 3.1   Social Structures and Types of Suicide

Social Structures	*Regulation*	*Regulation*
Integration	**Low**	**High**
High	Anomic suicide	Altruistic suicide
Low	Egoistic suicide	Fatalistic suicide

Types of Suicide

Anomic Suicide

When drastic changes occur in the norms and values of a society, the rules and regulations of that society will also change. For example, consider the Great Depression of the early 1930s in the United States. Almost overnight, some people lost their entire fortune. For some, the way they lived and the structure of their lives were changed forever. Some could not handle that change and chose to kill themselves. Stories were rampant about people jumping to their death from office windows.

Other scenarios exist where one can experience a rapid decrease in station, status, or finances, but a person can also experience a rapid rise in power and glory, such as the athlete who labors for years learning and acquiring the skills necessary to excel in a sport and then becomes an instant millionaire. A singer might become an overnight sensation. How does one handle the adulation and attention? For some, these pressures are too great, and they feel that suicide may be their only method of escape. The social pressures on them are too extreme, and their personal resources have either greatly diminished or grown to the point that their lifestyle has changed drastically.

In examining the role of a drastic change in economic status, several researchers (Breed, 1963; Gibbs & Porterfield, 1960; Henry & Short, 1954) found in their studies that although both upward and downward mobility are associated with suicide, suicide is more associated with downward mobility.

Altruistic Suicide

In this form of suicide, the person is seen as of little or no consequence; rather, the goal of the group is more important. The integration of the person with the group becomes so strong that an individual life is not important. What is important is the cause.

An example of this type of suicide is the person who offers his or her life for a social, personal, or religious cause. During the Vietnam conflict, more than one Buddhist monk knelt in front of a government building, poured gasoline over his body, and set himself on fire. By doing so, the monks hoped to call attention to the war and its alleged atrocities, the innocent people who suffered and were killed, and other actions of a predatory government against those people who emerged as "collateral damage."

It is apparent that a person who commits altruistic suicide suffers from a lack of individuation as well as a lack of social integration. What really matters? The cause! Does the person matter? Not at all. Altruistic suicide is much different from the other forms of suicide that Durkheim developed.

Egoistic Suicide

In egoistic suicide, a cause is not important. The center of the universe is the individual. This person is often bored with life, or as George Sanders, the actor, once said, he had done all there was to do and had seen all there was to see, and he was simply tired of living.

One young man left a suicide note that stated, in part,

> I cannot return to war. It is unjust. But I owe it to others by my own action [sic] to demonstrate the evil of our government, those power mongers who will sacrifice others for their own personal and financial gain.

As we can see, this form of suicide is the polar opposite of the altruistic suicide. In altruistic suicide, the cause is the reason to die; in egoistic suicide, the person is the central focus.

Fatalistic Suicide

A person who commits fatalistic suicide lives in a social structure that is hyperregulated. The person is in a situation from which he or she believes there is no escape, such as a woman who is in a marriage or partnership where abuse is frequent. This type of suicide is also seen in people who are terminally ill. Considering the cost of health care, any current or anticipated pain, or the knowledge that the family's financial resources will be depleted, the person may decide to commit suicide.

Box 3.1   Durkheim's Thoughts on Egoistic Suicide

- Rates of suicide will vary inversely with the strength of group regulation of members (e.g., family, religious institutions, and political groups).
- Rates of suicide will vary inversely with the strength of family integration. Durkheim assumes here that suicide rates will be higher among those who are divorced compared with those who are married, and higher for those who are single than for those who are married. Also, the suicide rate is higher for married individuals who have no children than for those who have children.
- Rates of suicide will vary inversely with the strength of religious integration. For example, Durkheim believed that the rate of suicide is higher for Protestants than for Catholics.
- Finally, Durkheim stated that the rates of suicide will vary inversely with political integration. He stated that political integration is weaker during peacetime; thus, suicide rates are higher.

Source: Farganis (2000), pp. 58–90.

The important component to this form of suicide is the feeling of being unable to escape the situation (see Figure 3.2). Durkheim maintained that fatalistic suicide examples also included those who led overregulated and *unrewarding* lives, such as slaves, young husbands caught for the first time in stressful financial and marital demands, and also childless married women. Liska (1987) found that men are more favorably affected by marriage than are women, and married men possibly are more socially integrated than women, especially in their younger years of marriage.

For whatever reason, Durkheim (1951) spent little time on the analysis or the explanation of fatalistic suicide. He believed that there were little incidences of fatalistic suicide in contemporary suicide (p. 276). As perhaps another example of fatalistic suicide, Treisman, Angelino, and Hutton (2001) are particularly alarmed that suicide may become more of a last resort for those with HIV. With approximately 1 million people now infected, the spread of this disease may dramatically affect the rate of suicide.

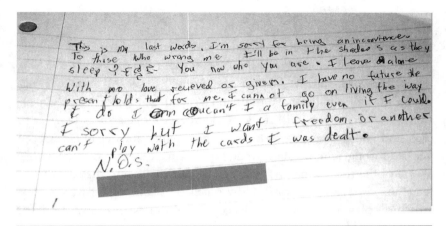

Figure 3.3

Selected Theories of Suicide

No one theory of suicide can explain such a complex chosen behavior. Biology, genetics, psychological traits, and social forces all play an important role in the decision to commit suicide. Many people attribute suicide to external circumstances, such as a breakup in a relationship, divorce, death, separation, loss of a job—but are these precipitating events or causes? Many people who kill themselves suffer from depression. Because depression and other mental illnesses so often underlie suicide (see Chapter 10), studying their causes is critical.

Biology and Suicide

Suicidal behavior often runs in families. If we accept this genetic predisposition, it may be that alcoholism, drug addiction, and other forms of destructive behavior have a biological basis.

This biological predisposition may also include a psychiatric profile that increases the risk for suicide. Certain parts of the brain may be affected in such a fashion that impulsive and violent behavior directed toward others may lead to violent behavior directed inward, such as attempted or completed suicide.

Psychology and Suicide

When he first developed initial psychological theories of suicide, psychoanalyst Sigmund Freud emphasized the role of hostility that was directed inward. Karl Menninger used Freud's ideas as a base and suggested that all suicides have three interrelated and unconscious dimensions: revenge/hate (a wish to kill), depression/hopelessness (a wish to die), and guilt (a wish to be killed). These dimensions have never been verified through empirical research, but they have served to make people aware of the role of the unconscious (as did Freud) and the role of violence that is directed inward. How much of a role these psychological structures play in a person's violence toward others and toward oneself is still debatable.

Edwin Schneidman (1991) described several common characteristics of suicides: unbearable psychological pain, a sense of aloneness and isolation, and a growing self-realization that death is the only solution to what Durkheim would call anomie. Other theorists emphasize the role of inflexible thinking and an inability to seek or complete solutions to problems.

Can it be that with some of those who commit suicide, especially the elderly, the act may be just a subjective, rational response to old age and the unique problems associated with growing old? Many people fear the deterioration of the physical abilities of the body, illnesses and disease, social isolation, social insults, and so on, coupled with a learned dread of decreased cognitive functioning (Draper, MacCuspie-Moore, & Brodaty, 1998; Margo & Finkel, 1990; Rubio, Vestner, Wilhelmsson, & Alleback, 2001). When cognitive functioning diminishes (Schneidman, 1991), the accompanying feelings of depression (Conwell, Duberstein, & Caine, 2002) and hopelessness (Conaghan & Davidson, 2002), as well as advancing personality problems (Clark, 1993; Maltsberger, 1991; Sadavoy, 1988) and anticipated losses (Achté, 1998; Draper et al., 1998), may all play an integral role in a person's decision to commit suicide. Minkoff, Bergman, Beck, and Beck (1973) say that many older and even not so old people may believe that nothing will go right; they will not be successful at anything; and the problems now confronting them will never get better, only worse. In addition, as Brown, Beck, Steer, and Grisham (2000), Conaghan and Davidson (2002), and Heisel (2004) all report that hopelessness becomes an important factor in the decision to commit suicide. In a study by Goodwin et al. (2003), the authors reported that suicide risk was higher when a bipolar patient was being treated with certain drugs as opposed to others. For example, they reported the risk of suicide was seven times higher when the patient was treated with the drug divalproex than it was for patients treated with lithium. This obviously has great implications for the physician involved in working up a medical plan for this kind of patient. In another study, Jick, Kaye, and Jick (2004) reported an interesting finding concerning the use of antidepressants and suicidal ideation. There was a substantial difference in the effects of some antidepressant drugs and suicide, especially on people between the ages of 10 to 19.

A novel theory in the suicide literature is the "escape theory" (Baumeister, 1990), which says that suicide is the end result of a series of events from which the person believes there is no escape. The escape theory holds true for both young and old alike, and it appears to have some of the elements of Durkheim's fatalistic suicide. But what makes this theory different is that it involves the person examining his or her life and how that life has not measured up to the expectations once held. This may be especially true for those who are elderly, because in the youthful and middle-aged populations, people may feel that there is still time to work on fulfilling those dreams and expectations, whereas the elderly may feel there is little time left.

Regardless of the theory or the reason, some people believe that many suicide attempts are symbolic cries for attention. Many people who are successful in their suicide attempts had tried it in the past. Was the first or second try a cry for help, and the final time successful because the person was now in earnest? This certainly deserves more attention. Will theories better prepare us to reduce the rate and scope of suicide? Is there a better place to start?

Religion and Suicide

Although studies have shown that religious people have a low rate of suicide, this statement is inherently problematic (Durkheim, 1951). It is very difficult, if not impossible, to validate empirically a person's religious commitment; what is easier to measure is church attendance.

However, if we can make the leap between church attendance and personal religiosity (the degree of participation in the beliefs and doctrine of a religion), then it indeed may be true that religion and spirituality (the quest for life's meaning and purpose) play an important and integral role in deciding *not* to commit suicide (Hovey, 1999; Siegrist, 1966; Stack & Lester, 1991). In addition, the strength of a person's belief in God, and whether that person was reared in a home with a religious bent, also factor into the decision (Comstock & Tonascia, 1978; Kark et al., 1996; Lester, 1992; Neeleman & Lewis, 1999).

If we examine the issue internationally, Neeleman (1998), in a study in the Netherlands, reported that religiosity, religious affiliation, and a firm religious system (one that is characterized by a clear and unchanging dogma) play integral roles in a decision to commit suicide. This same finding was also reported for countries in Scandinavia.

Clarke (2003) looked at urban versus rural settings and found that urban dwellers were less religious than rural dwellers and also had a higher rate of suicide. Females who were urban dwellers and more religious than men in the same locale were also less likely to commit suicide than their male counterparts.

We have found in our own study of suicide victims, from January 2003 to January 2004, that people who attended church regularly were six times less likely to commit suicide than those who did not attend religious services (Holmes & Holmes, 2004).

But what do organized religions teach their followers about suicide? The Christian attitude toward suicide probably emanates from the story of Judas, an apostle of Christ. His suicide was reported by the early church fathers as an act of despair; he had abandoned hope and thus his faith in God to forgive him. Recently, the Episcopal Diocese of Newark, New Jersey, reiterated the belief that suicide is always a grave offense and a personal affront to God, the giver of life. The Roman Catholic Church traditionally has opposed suicide. Historically, the person who committed suicide could not be offered mass or burial in consecrated ground. This stance has softened only in the past 20 years, as many in the Church have come to realize that people who commit suicide must have some inner compulsion (e.g., depression) or an external circumstance (e.g., terminal illness, debilitating pain) that factored into the decision. Similar to the Episcopalians, Muslims believe that suicide is an assault on human life, and it is to be condemned because it is a sacrilegious act, a defiance of God's will, and a denial that life is a sacred trust. The Jewish faith has also historically taken a strong stand against suicide. Whereas all major faiths believe that to offer one's life for God or a supreme ruler is laudatory, they have proscriptions against arbitrarily committing suicide because of poor present circumstances.

It is fair to say that most religions today leave some room for the person who commits suicide to escape personal responsibility for that action. For example, the Catholic faith now permits the person to be buried in hallowed ground. On the other hand, the Amish and Mennonites still believe that the person who has chosen suicide has turned his or her back on God and forfeits everlasting salvation (J. Williams, personal interview, March 12, 2005).

Thus, it is apparent that religion—at least church attendance—plays a critical role in a person's propensity to commit suicide. When one also considers gender, locale, and other social core variables, it becomes apparent that religion plays a critical role in that final decision.

Conclusion

Durkheim's work on suicide has been the most influential endeavor of all researchers analyzing the role of social structure and its influence on suicide. Needless to say, some researchers believe that his work has little value, and Durkheim's work does not really support the strong relationships suggested in his writing (Chambliss & Steele, 1966; Henry & Short, 1954; Pope, 1976). But even with the criticisms leveled against Durkheim, his work has brought attention to the role of social constraints and integration as important elements in suicide. As Liska (1987) says, "In emphasizing these factors [of a social nature], psychologists and psychiatrists have frequently neglected the social world. Durkheim . . . reminds us that the nature of the social order and people's integration in it are equally important" (p. 45).

We do know that many other theories of suicide exist besides Durkheim's. The works of Edwin Schneidman, Karl Menninger, and others need to be considered as we will undoubtedly continue to investigate the causes, traits, behaviors, and consequences of suicide.

4

Youth and Suicide

The adolescent years carry with them much discord and mayhem, some more dismal and dramatic than others. The cares and responsibilities for those who are in their late formative years may seem to be unlike those experienced by any other person in the world. Homelessness, drug abuse, and impulsivity all play some role in suicidal ideation (Dulcan, 2003). Zametkin, Alter, and Yemini (2001) go even further, asserting that the youth who kill themselves usually have an underlying psychiatric disorder. There have always been youth with no home, with drug dependence, and with psychological problems, but is the problem of youth suicide larger now than in past years? This question and others will be examined in this chapter.

Historically, research has shown that suicide is more of a societal concern with the elderly than the young. The rates and patterns are traditionally lower with youth than with the elderly. In recent years, however, this has changed. Youth and suicide are now becoming more of a concern. This is especially true for children 10 to 14 years of age (Stockard & O'Brien, 2002). It may be very common for teens, for example, to think about death and dying. Maybe it is because they are now thinking in a much different fashion; their maturity has allowed them to think more philosophically about their place in the world, the meaning of life, and other important and vital issues of life.

Recently, two young teens completed their suicide pact. Neither was a particularly close friend of the other in high school, but they made a promise to each other that they would commit suicide after school one afternoon. One young student shot the other and then turned the gun on herself. Neither had a fatal disease; their lives were

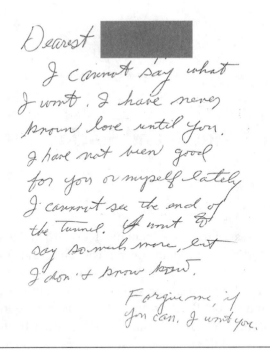

Dearest ▓▓▓▓▓
I cannot say what
I want. I have never
known love until you.
I have not been good
for you or myself lately
I cannot see the end of
the tunnel. I want to
say so much more, but
I don't know how.

Forgive me, if
you can. I want you.

Figure 4.1   Suicide note written by a 17-year-old to his girlfriend. They had just broken off their relationship.

simply not as they should be, and death was their answer. And of course, one question always seems to be a part of this type of suicidal behavior: Is there life after death?

The highs and lows of the teenage years permeate the mind-set of the young person (see Figure 4.1). Thinking about death, the toils of life, the meaning of life, feelings of helplessness, and the absence of power even over one's daily life all appear to be consequences of being a teenager. But the suicide act becomes most serious when a plan is made and put into action.

> *No one knew that Mike was depressed. He loved his car and worked throughout the summer to make money to fix it. He raked leaves, did odd jobs, and did any type of work he could find. But as the summer went on, he drew all of his money from the bank and gave it all to his friends. When all the money was gone, he killed himself.*

What are the causes of youth suicide? What is the extent of the problem? How do social and familial issues and problems affect youth? Heim et al. (2000) argued that there are medical reasons for a teen's propensity toward suicide. The authors stated that stress in a youth's life results in a persistent sensitization of the hypothalamic-pituitary-adrenal axis to stress in later life that may contribute to vulnerability to psychopathological conditions. These conditions may make some youth particularly susceptible to suicide. How accurate this hypothesis is depends on additional research that can attest to its validity and reliability. Perhaps what we need is a more comprehensive plan than we have now to understand the risks of suicide among youth (Gould, Greenberg, Velting, & Shaffer, 2003). And should we involve more social service agencies, law enforcement agencies, mental health agencies, and the total medical community? Phillips and Carstensen (1986) studied exposure to television news stories about suicide and the suicide rate. Their findings indicate that when a network carried a story about suicide in its evening programs, there was an increase in teenage suicides. Youth suicide rates were higher than adult suicide rates (6.87% vs. 0.45%). Phillips and Paight (1987), a year later, reported that when certain variables were controlled in their study and compared with previous studies, there was no difference in the suicide rate. They studied television movies that contained stories of teenage suicide. As often happens, their recommendations offered additional research, and any direct reporting of a contributing factor would be premature at this point. So does exposure to the media's stories of suicide have an effect on youth and their interest in and commission of suicide? These and other questions are of concern in this chapter.

Statistics on Suicide

According to the American Association of Suicidology, suicide among youth (ages 15–19) ranks as the third leading cause of death (see Table 4.1). This means that the suicide rate for this age group is 12 suicides for every 100,000 adolescents!

It appears that the overall suicide rate for young people has been slowly growing in the past 20 years, up until about 4 years ago, at which point it began to decrease slowly. The suicide rate for those in

Table 4.1   Suicide Rate per 100,000 Youth in the United States by Year, 1995–2000

Age	1995	1996	1997	1998	1999	2000
10–14	1.75	1.57	1.59	1.65	1.24	1.51
15–19	10.40	9.74	9.45	8.89	8.18	8.15

Source: Sourcebook of Criminal Justice Statistics Online, Table 3.139. Available: http://www.albany.edu/sourcebook/tost_3.html

the 15–19 age cohort increased only slightly in the past 20 years, but the suicide rate among the younger group (10–14) increased 99% during the same time, from .76 in 1980 to 1.51 in 2000. We will discuss methods of suicide later in this chapter, and we will see that firearms play a large role in the commission of suicide among the young.

Gender is also a significant differentiator among those youth who commit suicide. For example, in both age cohorts, the gender differences are the same: Four males commit suicide for every one female. Race is also an interesting factor to examine. White youth continue to commit suicide much more frequently than other ethnic groups (American Association of Suicidology, personal communication, November 15, 2003). We will discuss this factor further later in the chapter. Differences also exist among older youth who commit suicide regarding factors of family psychopathology, substance abuse, and greater suicide intent.

UNICEF reports that the United States ranks close to the middle range of reporting nations in youth suicide (Youth Suicide League, 2003). Finland, New Zealand, and Canada rank ahead of the United States.

Statistics do not tell us everything about the suicide problem. They give us a glimpse of the reported extent of the problem, but the human side of this problem needs to be examined from social and other perspectives.

Family Stability and Suicide

The family is the cradle for socialization. From the family, the child receives not only the biological building blocks for personality development but also, from the social milieu of parents and siblings, scripts for proper behavior and appropriate skills for life survival. It should be no great surprise that the stability of the family weighs heavily on the social and behavioral development of the young person. This is especially true for the youth who contemplates and commits suicide. Brent, Baugher, Bridge, Chen, and Chiappetta (1999) reported in their study of 140 youth suicide victims that parental pathology played a major role in a youth's decision to end his or her life.

Nelson, Farberow, and Litman (1988) and Wardarski and Harris (1993) reported that family disruption and the instability that exists within the family accounts for one of the leading factors in youth suicide. Larson and Larson (1990) reported that when a divorce occurs, the probability of youth suicide is much higher than when the family remains intact. Zweig, Phillips, and Lindberg (2002) reported that in a family where the levels of discord and stress are low, the risk of suicide is also low. They found that other factors, such as sexual promiscuity, drug use, and involvement in risk-taking behavior, also play a large role in attempted and completed suicides of the young person. Greene and Ringwalt (1996) reported that the influence of the family and the lack of stability play a great role in developing the mind-set of a youth contemplating suicide. Hayes (2000) found in her sample of juveniles in correctional custody that family discord, family abuse, and other forms of abuse within the family all play an integral part in the decision to attempt suicide. Incest may also factor into a youth's decision. How important is it? This may be very difficult to evaluate because getting the incestuous caretaker to disclose is often difficult (Morrison, 1988). This issue will be discussed further later in this chapter.

A 17 year-old young man wrote a suicide note to his parents:

Why did I do this? I am a coward. Right now, I'm already dead inside. I've been afraid of so much for so long. Video games have been a large portion of my life. Whenever I didn't like something, I would hit the off button. To put it in the most simplistic, and yet crude way possible, I had to hit the off button. Despite what you may think of me, I have never come close to having a girlfriend. I have been lucky enough to be friends with some interesting, humorous girls. I supplemented my relationships with porn, lots of porn. My magazine and DVD selection may be limited, but the internet provides fast and easy access to the women of my dreams. I became dependent on the internet for all the FREE material it would provide. Much like a video game. I could just turn off anything I didn't like.

I'm sick in the head. I've betrayed your trust. In the past year I've come to realize how great parents the two of you are. You've given so much. You've sacrificed so much for me and all I've given you is embarrassment, bills, and a loss to grieve. . . . I hope you somehow understand and even forgive me for what I am about to do.

The young man took his father's rifle and shot himself in the head.

Concerning family instability, Greene and Ringwalt (1996) stated that runaway youth have a distinct affinity for suicidal ideation. Runaways are frequently involved in various forms of substance abuse, and because this form of abuse is directly related to youth suicide, it holds a possible key for early identification of the problem and successful intervention.

Mental Health and Youth Suicide

Adolescents' mental health is vital when looking at suicide. How important is it? Hayes (2000) and Beyer (1998) reported that it is one of the most important factors to consider when developing a plan for intervention. Both authors revealed several risk factors in youth suicide, and mental health issues, such as intense loneliness, fear, self-blame, distrust, sadness, and hopelessness, were extremely important. Mental health professionals need to become integrally involved, not only in the treatment of suicidal youth, but also in the development of strategic plans to combat the problem of youth suicide. The National Center for

Injury Prevention and Control is concerned about this social problem and has developed a plan for intervention. This plan includes a national study to examine the scope of the problem; the risk factors; the development of intervention schemes; and the dissemination of information to professional mental health practitioners, law enforcement personnel, education professionals, and others to diminish the total number of incidences of youth suicide.

To illustrate the problem of lack of intervention with suicidal youths, the Substance Abuse & Mental Health Services Administration (SAMHSA, 2002) conducted a study of children ages 12 to 17. Those who had suicidal ideations during the past year were considered to be at risk. The Institute reported that more than 3 million youth were at risk for suicide. Their involvement with illegal drugs and alcohol contributed to their suicidal ideations. They also noted that within the at-risk group, only one in three received any counseling or mental health treatment.

Another risk group to consider is the many youths affected by the HIV/AIDS virus. Many live at home, but others live on the street. As Leary (1992) reported, HIV/AIDS merely compounds the problems these youth already have. Yet many youth deliberately place themselves in close proximity to the virus—a form of self-destructive behavior that needs to be addressed.

To further muddle the situation, it may be that race plays some part in the treatment and rehabilitation of youth who attempt suicide. For example, Huey et al. (2004) reported that family-centered, home-based intervention of those youth who had attempted suicide and were currently involved in a therapeutic program at the University of South Carolina were studied using race as one program element. Their results indicated that black youth did not benefit as much as white youth from the therapeutic treatment offered. However, even those youth who were psychiatrically challenged to a drastic degree benefited from treatment to lessen suicidal ideations.

Youth Suicide and Correctional Facilities

Literature that examines youth suicide in correctional facilities is sparse. Tartaro (2003) reported that most jail suicides among the general population of inmates occur within the first 24–48 hours. When suicides occur in a juvenile correctional facility, the administration and other involved professionals have to identify the risk factors in youth suicide. Penn, Esposito, Schaeffer, Fritz, and Spirito (2003) identified such risk factors as depression, anxiety, and anger, as well as self-mutilation, as indicators of suicidal behavior in juveniles. Depression is very difficult to diagnose because it may be more than simply a "down" state of mind. Some youth exhibit depression through a sense of sadness, hopelessness, social isolation, and low energy. Other young people may become rebels, runaways, truants, and drug abusers. Thus, depression can be symptomatic of other mental illnesses, including posttraumatic stress syndrome.

In Penn et al.'s study (2003), which sampled 289 juvenile residents, more than 12% had attempted suicide. If this number can be extrapolated to the total population of youth in correctional facilities in the United States, we can see that this is a huge problem. The identification of youth in correctional facilities with severe psychological problems needs special attention and treatment.

Youth Suicide and Substance Abuse

Substance abuse among youth is a monumental financial and social concern. Levy, Stewart, and Wilbur (1999) reported that the total cost of just alcohol abuse among the youth in this country was more than $200 per person or almost $600 per household. Alcohol, however, is just one type of drug, and other drugs play an equally detrimental role. For example, Greene and Ringwalt (1996) reported that youth who abuse sedatives, hallucinogens, and inhalants were more likely to attempt suicide. An additional finding, equally important, was that youth who come from families that abuse drugs were also more likely to commit suicide. Sabatino and Smith (1990) discovered that drug overdose is the most common form of youth suicide. Additionally, the risk of suicide increased when youth who were homeless also had homosexual sex (Remafedi, 2002). Yoder, Hoyt, and Whitbeck (1998) reported similar findings in their research with homeless and runaways in the Midwest. They reported that more than one in four youth attempted suicide. The number was much higher in the study by Kidd and Kral (2002); they found that more than 75% of their sample reported a history of attempted suicide. They also reported that drug abuse was a significant factor in the decision to attempt suicide, a finding also reported by Hayes (2000), and that the drugs themselves may be a form of slow suicide (Kidd & Kral, 2002). SAMHSA (2002) found that youth who were involved in illicit drug activity were very likely to have suicidal ideation.

Substance abuse plays a larger role in youth suicide among older adolescents than among younger adolescents (Brent et al., 1999). Thus for those who wish to intervene in youth suicide, the age of the substance abuser should be viewed as one more critical element in the suicidal process.

Substance abuse overdose is one of the top three methods of youth suicide (Laws & Turner, 1993). Because of the sheer numbers of youth who use drugs, including alcohol, this poses a monumental problem. What can be done? Education is certainly one strategy. But substance abuse may be an indicator of other, more serious problems in the youth's family or life. If those issues and concerns were dealt with, then maybe the substance abuse problem could be better understood and lessened.

To exacerbate the substance abuse problem, inhalants seem to be involved as a positive indicator of later suicides among users. Thompson, Franklin, and Eggert (2000) reported in their study of more than 1,200 high-risk and "typical" youth in high school that association with inhalants, alcohol, and marijuana led to the greatest risk of suicidal behavior. Thus, inhalant use can be considered a high predictor of later suicidal behavior. An added dimension of the inhalant issue was that those youth on inhalants were less likely to be supported by their care-takers and more likely to be runaways and homeless (Fletcher, Tortolero, Baumer, Vernon, & Weller, 2002).

Previous Attempted Suicides and Completed Suicides

In predicting suicide among youth, one of the most reliable indicators is a youth's previous suicidal behavior—the relationship between prior attempts and future attempts as well as completed suicides. Joiner,

Rudd, Rouleau, and Wagner (2000) found that such a relationship existed in their study of youth who had ideations and/or occurrences of attempted suicide. Of course, gender also plays a major role. Brent et al. (1999) reported that males chose weapons that were more likely to cause death than did females. They also reported that previous attempts at suicide were important indicators of another attempted or completed suicide.

Youth Suicide and Sexual and Physical Abuse

Sexual abuse and physical abuse significantly affect a youth's propensity to attempt suicide. Molnar, Shade, Kral, and Watters (1998) found that in their sample of 775 homeless youth, almost half of the females and more than 25% of the males had attempted suicide. The young women reported that they had attempted suicide at least six times, and the young men reported attempted suicide at least five times. Both genders reported significant episodes of physical abuse (both males and females = 35%), and 70% of the females reported sexual abuse whereas more than 20% of the males reported it. In examining both the groups—those who were homeless and abused and those who were homeless and not abused—the abused homeless group reported that they attempted suicide more than four times as often as the nonabused homeless group.

Physical abuse in a child has important implications for the youth's future behavior. There appears to be a direct relationship between youth who experience physical abuse at the hands of their caretakers and later suicide attempts or completions. Suicidal ideation becomes a by-product for many youths who experience such abuse (Straus & Kantor, 1991).

As Morrison (1988) pointed out, incest may play a vital role in a youth's decision to commit suicide. And because many of the incest perpetrators commit suicide after they are identified by the criminal justice system or the helping professions, attempting to understand what made them commit incest is impossible (Wild, 1988).

But the effects of incest may not always be a suicide predictor in the adolescent years. Peters and Range (1995) found in their study of sexually abused college students that females were more likely to have suicidal ideation than were males. Their general finding was that the college students who contemplated suicide and who were abused as a children were more likely to contemplate suicide than were those who did not experience such a traumatic event. Interestingly, women appear to have better coping skills with the aftereffects of incest than do men, at least in this one area.

Screening Programs and Youth Suicide

To identify youth with suicidal ideations, efforts have been directed toward the development of a self-report scale that would assess the most important known risk factors for suicide. For example, Gould et al. (2003) administered two tests to almost 2,000 high school students—the Columbia Suicide Screen and the Beck Depression Inventory. In examining the results of the tests, the researchers found that the predictors were not unanticipated. Previous suicide attempts and suicidal ideation were found to be the best indicators of a future attempt.

For high school students, this time in their lives appears to be very stressful. Drug abuse, unwanted pregnancies, peer pressure, and sexual abuse both in the home and on the dating scene all play some part in many teens' decisions to consider suicide. Silverman, Raj, Mucci, and Hathaway (2001) reported that rates of both physical and sexual dating violence; substance abuse; and other social, psychological, and medical issues common to teens play a very critical role in the decision to commit suicide.

Conclusion

Social institutions need to play a larger role in the identification and treatment of youth at risk for suicide. Schools, for example, have an essential role in the primary intervention process. A school could help develop a plan to raise the self-esteem of the youth, intervene with necessary and practical assistance in family pathological conditions and experiences, reduce the problems in the school environment that contribute to the lowering of self-esteem, and, in general, help develop a program to lower and eventually eradicate the problem of youth suicide (McEvoy & McElroy, 1994).

The criminal justice system can also help in the battle of youth suicide. With early identification of a child with significant risk factors, those within the system can use their experience and knowledge for proper referrals and identification of those in need (Zametkin et al., 2001).

Youth suicide is a societal problem. With the demands made on youth today in this society, we owe it to our children to explore better plans and strategies to intervene, help, and change young lives.

5

Suicide and the Elderly

On June 5, 2003, a 70-year-old man waited for his wife to go to sleep. He went outside, spread a blanket on the floor under his carport, and shot himself in the side of his head (see Figure 5.1). This elderly man was in the last stages of throat cancer. He had voiced his intentions several times to family members, and despite the protestations of his children, he was still bent on his own suicide. He said he suffered great pain from his cancer and wanted only to end his pain. His wife was in the intermediate stages of dementia and had little understanding of his situation. One of his final questions to his daughter was that if something did happen to him, would the children take care of her? She promised her father the family would.

Suicide and the Elderly

One 80-year-old man wrote in his suicide note, "Death is as much a reality as birth, growth, maturity, and old age—it is one certainty. I do not fear death as much as I fear the indignity of deterioration, dependence, and hopeless pain." He left this note on his kitchen table. His health had failed dramatically, he had lost almost his entire fortune to the nation's failing economy, his only son had been killed in a fatal motor vehicle accident, and his wife was in a nursing home with Alzheimer's disease and seldom recognized him despite his daily visits to the nursing home. For himself, he was fearful of being incapacitated and without the resources to live independently.

Figure 5.1   This elderly man with a history of heart trouble and throat cancer took his own life in the early morning hours. Notice the gun by his right foot. Investigation by the coroner's office determined he was kneeling when he shot himself.

He continued:

> If the time comes when I can no longer take part in decisions for my own future, let this statement stand as the testament of my wishes:
>   If there is no reasonable expectation of my recovery from physical or mental disability, I, [his name], request that I be allowed to die and not be kept alive by artificial measures . . .
>   Dear family, I cannot stand it anymore. I love you all.
>   Dad

Is this a form of fatalistic suicide? Probably. But it appears from our research that many of the elderly face the issue of suicide as their health deteriorates; their self-image falters; they lose their family members, including their spouse or partner; and other personal issues and dilemmas arise.

There is an old adage that says the older the person, the greater the wish to die. We will see later that there is a great deal of truth to this statement. It is especially true for men. Perhaps coupled with failing health, the loss of a productive image, and declining independence, these three elements play a vital role in the decision to commit suicide. Slatkin (2003), for example, remarks that because we have a society whose members are living longer, many diseases and personality and social disorders will become more prevalent. This will put more and more elderly people at risk. Thus, the rate of depression and alcohol

---

Box 5.1   Suicide and the Elderly

Approximately every 83 minutes, one adult 65 years of age or older commits suicide in the United States. The suicide rate for this age group rose by 9% between 1980 and 1992. During that period, there were 74,675 suicides by elderly people. In 1993, suicide rates ranged from 15 per 100,000 people 65 to 69 years old, to 24 per 100,000 people 80 to 84 years of age, a rate that is double the overall U.S. rate. White males are at nearly 10 times the risk for suicide as nonwhite males across the age spectrum.

White men over 80 years old are at the greatest risk of all age, gender, and racial groups. The suicide rate for this group is six times the current overall rate and three times the rate of African American males over 80 years old. This high rate among white males over 80 is important because the very elderly age group (85 years and older) is the fastest growing subpopulation of elderly adults in the United States.

Older adults tend to use highly lethal means to commit suicide. In 1988, nearly 8 out of 10 suicides committed by men 65 years and above used a firearm. Of the 6,363 elderly adults who committed suicide in 1988, for example, 67% (4,264) used firearms to end their lives. Hanging and poisoning were the second and third leading causes of suicide in this group.

Source: Institute on Aging, August 10, 2004. Available: http://www.nia.nih.gov/

and drug abuse will contribute to committing suicide. It may be that those in the criminal justice system as well as the helping professions need to be alerted to the special needs of the elderly as the American population ages.

As mentioned earlier, alcohol may play a role in the decision to commit suicide with many of the elderly. The consumption of alcohol provides a sense of peace, calm, and tranquility, so the act of taking one's

---

Box 5.2   Risk and Protective Factors in Suicide Among the Elderly

Risk Factors

Mental Pathologies—Various studies have shown that there is a relationship between severe mental pathologies and propensity toward suicide.

Significant and Sometimes Fatal Illnesses—For many people who are either severely or terminally ill, the only way to escape the pain, suffering, and financial difficulties is to commit suicide.

Alcohol and Drug Abuse—As will be discussed in a later chapter, there is a relationship between the abuse of alcohol and drugs and the decision to commit suicide. This abuse is often symptomatic of personal, mental, or emotional problems.

Previous Suicide Attempts—Perhaps one of the more telling indicators of another attempted suicide is the number of previous suicide attempts.

Family Issues and Problems—In many cases, partner or spousal separation or a relationship deterioration may prompt many to consider suicide. This is also true when a spouse or partner dies and the survivor cannot bear living without him or her. This is especially true for the elderly.

Career and Financial Losses—If a person's retirement has not been adequately planned as far as finances are concerned, or if other social or financial issues enter the planned retirement scenario, this can have a drastic and dramatic effect upon the person.

Social Losses and Isolation—As a person ages, he or she may experience a sense of loss when many of his or her friends, relations, and acquaintances die or are no longer there. Consequently, this support group no longer exists.

Anger and Personal Maladaptive Behaviors—Some people have developed such maladaptive behaviors that they find it very difficult to adjust to a world where personal conflicts are inevitable. To this type of person, the ultimate aggressive act is suicide.

Protective Factors

Weaponry Restrictions—In many cases, the choice of weapon is the handgun. With the elderly, it may be that access to guns, especially for males, may increase the possibility of suicide. Females, however, are more apt to use drugs, carbon monoxide, and cutting than handguns.

Family Support Systems—For many, not just the elderly, having a strong family system can certainly help prevent the possibility of a suicide. Warmth and a feeling of acceptance are certainly positive counterindicators for suicide.

Good Mental and Physical Health—As one ages, physical health often deteriorates. However, with good medical care, sound physical health can be maintained over a longer period of time. As stated in this chapter, there is a relationship between failing health and a decision to commit suicide. The same can be said regarding mental health status. With depression and other forms of psychological impairments, successful treatment can make a difference.

Elderly Self-Image and Perceptions—As one ages, self-image and perception can change. However, acceptance of aging and the benefits that age can bring can help a person view life's changes as being not only normal but also beneficial.

Social Involvement, Activities, and Personal Development—As a person ages and moves into the retirement phase of life, he or she will have opportunities to develop new interests, new friendships, and relationships. This can certainly have an influence on his or her happiness.

Financial Security—In the aging years, a properly planned financial program can ease a person's mind. Accepting that in some cases, investments may not materialize as planned, adequate financial resources can provide a sense of not only financial security but also personal security.

Source: Adapted from APA Online, July 26, 2004. Available: http://www.apa.org

---

Box 5.3   Signs of Alcoholism in the Elderly

- Frequent or daily use of alcohol
- Periods of lost time or amnesia while drinking
- Continuation of drinking after warnings to stop
- Physical signs of abuse of alcohol
- Altered cognitive abilities
- Anemia
- Liver abnormalities
- Frequent loss of physical abilities resulting in loss of control
- Seizure activity after a period of extensive alcohol abuse

Source: D. Hunsaker, personal interview, March 20, 2005.

Box 5.4   Suicide Attempts

For the population as a whole, approximately 25 suicide attempts occur for every death by suicide. Ratios for the young (24 years of age and younger) are as high as 200 attempts for every suicide. For elderly people, the ratio of attempts to completed suicides narrows dramatically to four attempts for every suicide. Thus, an older person who contemplates suicide is more likely to complete the act, for several reasons. First, as mentioned previously, elderly people often employ more lethal methods when attempting suicide. Second, older people experience greater social isolation. Finally, the elderly generally have poorer recuperative capacity, which makes them less likely to recover from a suicide attempt.

Source: Institute on Aging, August 10, 2004. Available: http://www.nia.nih.gov/

---

life may feel more acceptable. Or, if the elderly person has a history of alcohol abuse, that may exacerbate the personal and social problems present in his or her life.

Box 5.3 contains information that is often present in many, if not most, alcoholics. But it may be especially true for elderly alcoholics. The physical signs are more pronounced as a person ages because the body has had time to process the disease and succumb to the consequences of it.

Types of Elderly Suicide

When we speak of suicide among the elderly, it is apparent that not all the elderly will commit suicide for one reason. The American Medical Association (AMA) offered a typology of suicide among the elderly ("Knowing Reasons for Suicide," 2003). Acknowledging that many of the elderly will commit suicide because of depression or loneliness, or because they feel less important, or perhaps because their health is declining, the AMA found in its research that these ideas may not necessarily be true. The AMA's research led to the following typology.

Not Distinctively Elderly Suicides

The AMA's study determined that the majority of elderly suicides were not related to age-specific issues, such as depression, anomie, and failing health. It stated that the information received from interviews with those who attempted suicide was not fundamentally different from suicides of 30-, 40-, or 50-year-olds. Thus, there is nothing intrinsically different motivationally about elderly suicide.

Protest Suicides

Each person's life has milestone points in the aging process, and these points offer different challenges and demands. In the AMA's study, the researchers identified a group of people who were not able to be flexible and could not adapt to the changes brought about by the aging process. These people might get extremely agitated because of their forgetfulness or lack of physical mobility, and because they cannot accept normal physical changes, they react with some type of suicidal ideation, even to the point of committing suicide.

Preemptive Suicides

A person who commits preemptive suicide does so after experiencing a particularly disturbing death of a loved one or a friend because he or she does not want to go through the same experience. This preemptive "strike" could be triggered by an illness or a presumed illness. This type of suicide is akin to Durkheim's fatalistic suicide type, mentioned earlier.

Box 5.5   Underreporting of Suicides

Minimum estimates of suicides among the elderly in the United States range from 6,000 to 10,000 annually. Often, these suicides are not reported as such but are listed as accidental deaths. Many are committed by isolated, lonely older people. In some cases, there are no friends or family members who care about the person's death; in other cases, if there are friends or family, they may be too afraid to inquire about the nature of the death because of the stigma attached to suicide. Additionally, suicides are often mistaken for natural deaths, especially in cases of medicinal overdosing, because many older people take several medications.

Source: Institute on Aging, August 10, 2004. Available: http://www.nia.nih.gov/

Are typologies such as the AMA's valuable? They may give us some understanding as to the type of person likely to commit suicide. They may also give those in the helping professions a better understanding of the special concerns and issues that aging has for suicide.

Elderly Suicide and Statistics

In examining the data provided by the *Sourcebook of Criminal Justice Statistics Online,* the following statistics are readily apparent:

- Although the elderly make up less than 15% of the population, they account for more than 25% of all suicides.
- More than 75% of the elderly who committed suicide saw their primary care physician in the month before their suicide.
- Males account for more than six times as many elderly suicides as females.
- Men over age 85 are at the highest risk category for suicide.
- The suicide rate for women over the age of 65 does not appear to increase as the women get older.

Table 5.1 contains data concerning age, gender, race, and suicide. It is readily apparent that, across racial boundaries, males commit suicide

Table 5.1   Suicide Rate (per 100,000 persons in each age group above 65) by Age, Race, and Gender, 2000

Age	White Male	White Female	Black Male	Black Female	Other Male	Other Female
65–69	21.73	4.44	8.97	0.56	7.64	3.20
70–74	27.88	4.45	12.75	1.36	15.28	3.22
75–79	36.46	3.99	11.38	1.47	20.52	5.29
80–84	46.99	4.32	12.45	3.65	21.46	7.69
85+	58.76	4.52	11.71	0.44	29.81	6.74

Source: National Center for Injury Prevention and Control (2003). Available: http://www.cdc.gov/ncipc/default.htm

more often than females in the elderly cohort. Racially, the numbers jump dramatically as a person reaches the age cohort of over 85. Females stay relatively stable at that point with the exception of black females over 85, whose suicide rate drops drastically.

What are some reasons for this increase in the wish to die as one grows older? For the male, it may be a combination of several things. First of all, as one grows older, a person's health generally decreases. And because people are now generally living longer, their living conditions may have a detrimental effect on their mental health. The combination of changing and isolated conditions of many of the elderly, their changing and deteriorating health conditions, and the deterioration of a positive self-image all contribute to suicidal ideation.

Females do not seem to be as affected by aging as far as suicide is concerned. Women's suicide rates are more consistent. Black females seem to be more consistent in their suicide rates as the rates get higher, and they peak in the age cohort 80–84 before decreasing in the last age grouping, 85+ years. Generally speaking, the aging process has an effect upon one's decision to end one's life. Regardless of the reason, be it health, isolation, marital problems, spouse's general health, or something else, elderly suicide is a real concern.

We need to be careful, though, in the acceptance of statistics regarding suicide and the elderly. Using the term *silent suicide,* Simon (1989) calls attention to the fact that many more suicides occur in the elderly than are commonly suspected. For example, many elderly people try to kill themselves through self-starvation or noncompliance with medication. In these cases, death investigators may miss the suicide and call the death accidental or natural. Simon adds that the elderly person who completes this form of suicide is not thought to be suffering from depression or some other form of debilitating condition.

Elderly Suicide and Physical Health

Age often brings with it physical deterioration as well as a propensity for diseases and illnesses. What this does to the mental state of the elderly person with suicidal ideation is well documented. For those who are in the final stages of a terminal disease, the feelings of hopelessness and aloneness may become such influencing factors that suicide would be a welcome escape.

Lest we believe that the elderly succumb to suicide only when they are in the final stages of a fatal disease, one study shows that only 2% to 4% of suicide victims have been diagnosed with a terminal illness at the time of their death (Alexopoulos, Bruce, Hull, Sirey, & Kakuma, 1999). Additionally, almost one victim in five visited a physician the day before committing suicide! Three out of four of those who successfully committed suicide saw their primary care physician in the month prior to their death.

One elderly man stated,

> I am tired of living. I have had a good life, married the girl of my dreams, and had three beautiful children. I am ready now to meet her as well as my mother and father in the next life. Please forgive me for what I am about to do. I love you all.
> Dad

The brother of this man was interviewed. He stated that his brother was a psychologist who was well-liked and well-respected both personally and professionally. He had lived in the community all of his life. He was recently widowed after more than 40 years of marriage. The brother said that since his wife died, his brother "had never been the same."

It may be that the assumed consequences of a debilitating illness, or the loss of a significant other, are the more weighty issues in an

Figure 5.2

elderly person's decision to commit suicide. For example, many elderly people do not wish to be a burden to their children and other caretakers. In the research from our own cases, we have found that many of the elderly who leave suicide notes or letters mention health as one of the major contributing factors in their decision. For these people, committing suicide while one is still capable of making that decision may become a compelling reason to take that step. Many people mention, for example, that they do not wish to spend their last days in a nursing home, or be in a situation in which they are not able to control their own fate. Where once they were able to function on their own, the lack of ability to do so becomes an overwhelming concern.

Elderly Suicide and Psychological Health

As many as 2 million Americans aged 65 and over suffer from some type of depression (Alexopoulos, 2000; Narrow, 2000). Depression is an

---

Box 5.6   Selected Cases of
Homicide and Suicide Among the Elderly

In Seaside, New Jersey, an elderly couple, 74 and 72, bound themselves with speaker wire and walked into the ocean. The wife apparently died of hypothermia, but the husband survived. A suicide note was found by the investigators. The missive stated, in part, that they were depressed and wanted to die together. The wife had been in poor health for the past several months.

In Roxbury, New Jersey, a man, 92, was apparently upset over the death of his friend. He placed a plastic bag over his wife's head and suffocated her. The wife was unable to thwart the attack. The man then took a knife from the kitchen and thrust the knife into his chest, killing himself.

What made this case so difficult to understand was that the couple had no history of domestic violence. They had apparently been happily married for 60 years, and neither was terminally ill nor had any drastic history of illness or hospitalization.

In Louisville, Kentucky, a 78-year-old man and his 75-year-old wife were found by their son in the couple's car, parked inside their garage. The son had not heard from them in the past 5 days. The couple were sitting the car, a cell phone between them, and holding hands. The wife had been hospitalized for cancer and was considered terminal. They both died of carbon monoxide poisoning.

---

atypical state of mind. There are normal reactions to emotional depression, which is a state of mind after some real or imagined loss. The loss of a partner, poor health, and loss of financial stability all present occasions for "normal" depression. But with some elderly, depression becomes all pervasive and enveloping. Depression that is ongoing and exceeds acceptable boundaries of appropriateness, especially when it occurs with other illnesses, must be treated. Intervention plays an important role and results in the treatment of depression and thus the reduction of suicide in the elderly (Bruce et al., 2004).

Table 5.2   Mental Health and Suicidal Tendencies Among the Elderly

Mentally Healthy

Those who had thought that life was not worth living	4%
Those who had had "death wishes"	4%
Those who had thought of suicide	0.9%
Those who had seriously thought of taking their own lives	0%

Mentally Disordered

Those who had thought that life was not worth living	29.2%
Those who had had "death wishes"	27.5%
Those who had thought of suicide	9.2%
Those who had seriously thought of taking their own lives	1.7%

Source: Skoog et al. (1996).

Depression is also linked to an elderly person's decision to commit suicide with the help of his or her physician (Blank et al., 2001). Aggressive intervention by medical professionals, including the primary care physician, can certainly reduce the risk of suicidal ideation and actual suicides. Included in this intervention should be an effective working plan that reduces the suicidal ideation process (Bruce et al., 2004).

As noted in Table 5.2, mental health plays an important and integral role in one's deliberations concerning suicide. For example, Skoog et al. (1996) found that one's mental health condition is statistically significant. In their study, they interviewed an elderly population regarding suicidal ideation in the past 30 days and found that elderly people with mental disorders had a much higher rate of suicidal ideation than did those without mental disorders. From their results, it is apparent that the state of mind is important and must be considered in the medical community's diagnoses and treatments of the mentally ill.

In a study by Bruce et al. (2004), researchers from Cornell and the University of Pittsburgh studied a sample of 600 elderly patients suffering from depression. They found that the patients who were exposed to structured treatment for their depression—treatment that included antidepressants, psychotherapy, or a combination of the two—were better able to resolve their feelings of depression and thus able to resolve their suicidal ideations.

Figure 5.3   In this case, an elderly man carefully displayed his bank
papers; insurance policies; and names, addresses, and phone
numbers of relatives. The man, a dentist, had been depressed
and decided to take his life.

What are the implications of such research? Simply stated, a suit-
able treatment modality can offer hope for the treatment of depressed
elderly who have suicidal ideations (see Figure 5.3). Of course, an additional problem needs to be addressed, and this is the early identification of such individuals.

For example, in March 2004, a man had not seen his 65-year-old
mother for the past week. He went to her home and found her dead.
She left several suicide notes to different family members. As Ron
Holmes was talking with the son, he called his brother and informed
him of their mother's death. He said that they should have suspected
something like this would happen because she had been depressed for
the past several years. She had been taking medication, all prescribed
by one physician. During the course of the interview with the son,

I asked him if the mother had seen a psychotherapist for her depression, and he replied that she had not. There needs to be a concentrated effort to educate physicians on the need for not only medication, but also some form of therapy in a structured program in order to circumvent suicidal ideation.

Conclusion

More research is needed if we are to combat the social problem of suicide and the elderly. It may be that medications and psychotherapies are needed for the person who is depressed and has suicidal ideation. The successful combination of both may be the best response for effective treatment.

Waern et al. (2002) believe that mental disorders play a large and probably the most important role in suicide in the elderly. Depression is one of the most common mental disorders and is often associated with suicide. Waern et al. also say that the elderly who commit suicide compose a heterogeneous group with regard to mental disorders, and special care needs to be directed to this group in order to reduce suicide within this age cohort.

6

Suicide and Violence Among Intimates

It may be that the family is a cradle of violence. There is a widespread belief that people learn to be violent because they see violent acts in their own families. Violence may be a learned process that is accompanied by a genetic predisposition for violence toward others and also oneself. Conner, Cerulli, and Caine (2002) found in their study of partner-violent men that these men demonstrated a heightened risk of suicide, and their suicidal threats increased as their court date approached. Additionally, those men who had either threatened or attempted suicide not only were more violent at the index offense, but also showed greater domestic violence severity overall.

> In 2003, Tacoma, Washington, _____ shot and killed his wife and then killed himself. _____ had a history of physical abuse and past allegations of rape and domestic violence.

Many factors are involved in family relationships and the propensity for homicide and suicide among those who are intimates. This is the focus of this chapter.

Violence Among Intimates

The number of violent crimes by male intimate partners against females declined from 1993 to 2001. These crimes ranged from simple assault to homicide. Simple assault was the most common form of domestic violence, and rape or sexual assault was the least common. Intimate violence, however, is a significant social problem. Intimate partner violence comprised 20% of all nonfatal crime experienced by women and 3% of the nonfatal violence against men (Rennison, 2003). As far as fatal violence is concerned, in 2000, 1,247 women and 440 men were killed by intimate partners.

Suicide has become almost common in the aftermath of fatal violence directed toward an intimate partner. As Conner et al. (2002) pointed out, in the case of domestic abuse, male perpetrators are more likely to commit suicide than is the general population. This is especially true as their court date approaches. This has important implications for the corrections profession when the alleged offender is in a correctional facility awaiting that date. Conner et al.'s research also suggested that men who commit acts of domestic abuse and exhibit suicidal ideation are also more likely to be involved in more severe acts of domestic physical and sexual abuse. Conner, Duberstein, Conwell, and Caine (2003) reported that in many partner relationships that culminated in homicide/suicide, relationship disruptions and psychiatric disorders played an important role in the decision to commit suicide.

Despite the fact that the number of domestic violence crimes has fallen in the past 10 years, it is still an important and grave problem. For example, since 1976, the number of male victims of intimate partners has dropped by 4%, and female victims by 1%. However, we should not be concerned only with percentages; the human cost to survivors, family members, relatives, and friends and acquaintances cannot be measured only in numbers.

Articles appear in the media every day about domestic homicides/suicides. This occurs not only in married couples but also in those who are in committed relationships or dating.

Recently, a 20-year-old female attempted to break up with her boyfriend. Despite her unwillingness to talk with him, he continued to

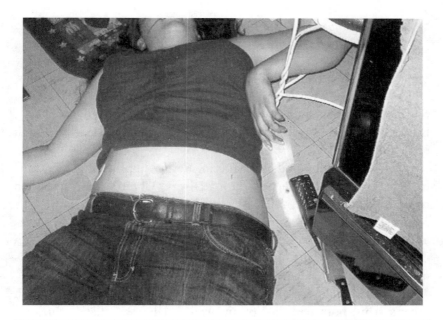

Figure 6.1   After this woman had taken out an emergency protective
                     order, her boyfriend broke into her home the next day and
                     killed her. He then killed himself.

stalk her and interfere with her daily routine, going to her work site,
following her when she was shopping, and calling her home continu-
ally. Finally, on a Friday, she went to the local court and took out an
emergency protective order against him. Finding the court order later
that day, he went to court and had the same legal document served on
her. The next afternoon, incensed, he drove to her suburban home,
broke in, and shot her one time in the heart (see Figure 6.1). Then, he
went into another room and shot himself under the chin. This was not
a fatal wound, so he shot himself a second time in the back of the head.
When the police and the coroner's office arrived, both were dead. He
was charged with homicide posthumously.

The above-mentioned case is not unique. And as Tjaden and
Thoennes (2000) report, violence among intimates may be more widespread than once thought.

Battered Partners,
Violence, and Partner Homicide/Suicide

Spouses are often battered, beaten, and murdered by family intimates, and as mentioned earlier, there is a relationship between violence in the family and suicide. For example, battered women who have a history of drug abuse also have an extremely high rate of suicide (Ragin et al., 2002).

Guns are seldom used as a battering device, but they are often used to kill. For example, the Centers for Disease Control and Prevention reported that in 2002, 58% of all suicides involved a firearm. The reported percentage of homicides involving some type of firearm was almost 40% (National Center for Health Statistics, 2002). Indeed, families are often the scene of much violence—not just battering and beatings, but also fatal violence.

As an example, Ian and Patricia England[1] were found dead in each other's arms; both had died of an overdose. Ian, a college professor, had suffered from depression for several years and was under the care of a psychiatrist. Patricia was also a college professor and fought a constant battle with obesity. Ian, from Ireland, had been arrested two times for domestic abuse, and Patricia had been treated in the hospital several times for broken bones, lacerations, and other minor injuries. Despite the violence in the family, relatives and friends said that the couple loved each other, and, as is typical of abusers, each time Ian abused his wife, he apologized profusely and promised not to do it again.

Neighbors said that the couple had a loud fight the weekend before their deaths. One neighbor said that she heard some furniture falling, but because this had happened several times in the past, she did not call the police.

Neither reported for work at their university, and Patricia's sister came to their home after attempts to call them failed. She found them in their bedroom on the floor next to the door (see Figure 6.2).

They had not left a suicide note. Recently purchased food sat in the refrigerator, and ample supplies were in the pantry. The couple had two birds in a large cage, and the birds had plenty of food as well. Their families had no notion that Ian and Patricia were thinking of

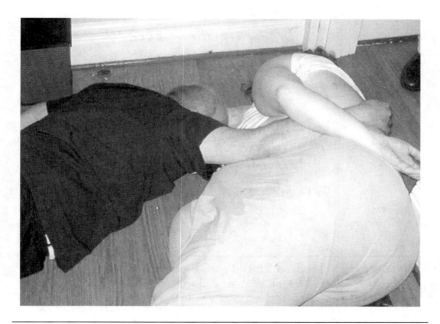

Figure 6.2   The couple committed suicide by an overdose of prescription drugs. The man was terminated recently from his part-time teaching job.

suicide. Both were completely devoted to each other, the relatives stated, despite his violent temper and their problems with the criminal justice system, and they seemed willing to end their lives in each other's arms.

Ragin et al. (2002) report an association between abuse and attempted suicide. Within the family setting, abuse can take many forms, including physical, sexual, and substance abuse. And of course, violence in the family can result not only in physical altercations, but also in death.

Sarah and Mike Adams[2] had a long history of domestic violence. Mike had repeatedly abused Sarah, resulting in physical injuries. They fought many battles for many different reasons. Friends and relatives all said that they constantly argued about finances, friends, alleged affairs, and other things. Sarah often called her best friend to tell her that Mike had hit her again, and she would add that she did not know

To Whom It May Concern.
She was not a nice
person. I did it. I guess
I can't live without
her.
    Tell Mom and Buddy
goodby.

Figure 6.3   The husband left this suicide note. After he shot his wife to death, he took the gun and shot himself in the temple. Both were dead at the scene. The note was left in the kitchen.

---

how much longer she could take it. Mike, on the other hand, said that he loved his wife, and despite their violent differences, he did not think he could ever leave her and could not bear the thought of living without her. Finally, as often happens, their last fight occurred, and it ended with Sarah's homicide and Mike's suicide (see Figure 6.3).

As Breault has pointed out, marriage may certainly intensify the problems and concerns that exist within a family. In other words, there are preexisting emotional and social problems that may lead one to homicide and suicide (K. Breault, personal communication, May 10, 2004).

In another case, a 28-year-old man became despondent over the loss of his 22-year-old girlfriend. She started dating another young man and refused to go out with him. He waited until the couple came home from a date, approached them in the parking lot at her apartment, and shot both of them multiple times.

Intimate partners occur in different types of relationships, such as marriage or dating. Emotional ties are typically strong and deep. When these ties are somehow threatened—whether that threat is real or imagined—some people will commit suicide (see Figure 6.4), whereas other people commit homicide before killing themselves (see Table 6.1).

Figure 6.4   A 20-year-old male was despondent over his girlfriend leaving him. They had been in a highly volatile relationship for the past 2 years. The couple had visited each other the night before his suicide, and she told him that she was finally leaving him for another man and he could not see his daughter. He hung himself in the back yard. His note expressed great hostility toward his ex-girlfriend, the mother of his child.

Table 6.1   Murder Victims of an Intimate Partner

	Male		Female	
Year	Number	Percent of All Murders	Number	Percent of All Murders
1976	1,357	9.6	1,600	34.9
1980	1,221	6.9	1,549	29.6
1990	859	4.7	1,501	29.3
1993	708	3.7	1,581	28.5
2000	440	3.7	1,247	33.5

Source: Federal Bureau of Investigation (various years) and http://www.ojp.usdoj.gov/bjs/homicide/intimates

Sadly enough, on some occasions, a person will commit suicide after killing his or her children. That person may believe that he or she is removing the children from a life of torture, pain, and suffering. Certainly, many people, especially women, are so constrained financially that they cannot fend for themselves, and they must depend on an abusive mate for survival. It may be that they have not been trained or educated for financial survival, or have no family support or ties; thus, the abusive mate is their only recourse.

In another case, a 42-year-old man decided to end his life because of a relationship gone wrong. The content of his letter does not make clear the exact nature of the real or imagined transgression committed by his partner in this case, but it was enough for him to commit suicide.

> *To my dear family, I am so sorry for what I have done.*
>
> *I know my actions make no sense to you now and my [sic] never but I have failed you, my peers and myself in a way I never thought possible.*
>
> *Having lead [sic] a life that most everyone would be proud of, accomplishing things I only dreamt of as a kid and having the respect for the life I lead and the professional I became at work, I cannot bare [sic] my future. I known [sic] I would never smile again, enjoy a laugh, or be able to look anyone in the eyes again, so my "life" is over.*

The loss I feel for the joys I will never have is overwhelming. The joy of spending time with each of you, my dear brother and best friend, my sisters who I adore and my nieces and nephews who I am the proudest uncle is my greatest loss. Dad, I am so sorry to disappoint you.

To all my coworkers who's [sic] respect I value daily and the pride I took working with you, I will miss you all.

To _____, my great friend, I will miss your laugh and fun we have had, I cannot express my disappoint [sic] I myself and could not bare [sic] to tell you my failing.

To _____, it has been an honor working for and with you; we have had some great accomplishments. Not seeing the completion of our build-ing is hugely disappointing; it was a project I was most proud of.

A brief explanation: More than 4 years ago, a women [sic] joined our company, she lives in Orlando. On every occasion we had need to meet on business she made advances which I would tell her each and every time this could not and will not happen. I knew she was with another man. Yet she persisted. Last summer she started contacting me at home under the pretence [sic], as I see it now, to help me through a difficult year. After 7 or 8 months she gained my trust and it devel-oped into what I thought was a valuable friendship. She convinced me that I was the only one in her life and she took it to the next level, com-ing here last December, after that the contact continued with hours nightly on the phone. Last weekend we met in Florida, something I had never done before. I trusted her, believed her and now I have lost everything. I learned on Monday, from someone else she is having a relationship with, that everything was a lie. She is not the caring, thoughtful person I thought I knew. I was deceived, her past and cur-rent relationships with someone in our industry was not what she told me, she is not the person I spent hours on the phone with. It is all so overwhelming I am shaken to the core of my being. I cannot face my future, she has put me in a position that I can never again succeed, and I will have lost all respect from my peers and now my family also. She has taken me from someone I was proud to be, to someone involved in a relationship that I now despise. I am ashamed of what I allowed to happen, and what I did. This is not me, yet I did it and for that I am forever sorry.

> *To everyone, most specially my family, I held what you thought of me at the highest regard and now I have lost that, you, my future happiness and now my life.*
>
> *Again I am so very sorry for my actions and the pain I have caused. I cannot express the depth. Please forgive me.*

The man went into his garage. He turned on his MP3 player and, after starting his car, sat on his steps and waited to die (see Figure 6.5).

What exactly was the critical issue with the woman is not known at this time. His family is not aware of the identity of the woman, and his business partner was also unaware of any possible conflict. Regardless,

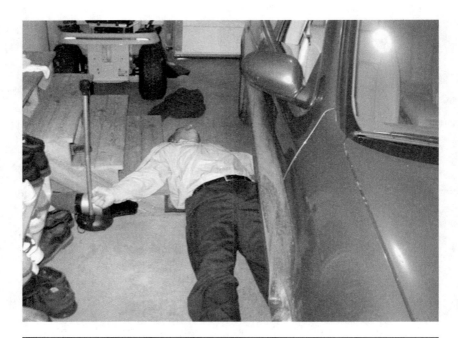

Figure 6.5   When the ambulance responded to the scene, this suicide victim was lying on his side, off the steps. Emergency medical workers placed him supine to administer emergency aid.

the nature of their relationship threatened to bring him shame, something he would rather die than face.

What to Look for in Older Adults and Homicide/Suicide

In domestic violence and homicide-suicide among older people, certain behavioral and social clues are typically observed. Cohen (2004) lists the following:

1. The couple has been married for a long period of time, and the husband has a dominant personality.

2. The husband is the primary caregiver, and the wife has a debilitating disease.

3. One or both has a serious and perhaps fatal disease.

4. A move to an assisted living center is imminent.

5. The couple is becoming more socially isolated from family, friends, and acquaintances.

6. Separation or divorce is possible.

7. Because the husband is usually the killer, the following warning signs should be noted:

   - Changes in eating or sleeping
   - Crying for no apparent reason
   - An inability to feel good about the future
   - Talk of feeling hopeless
   - Talk about the future as bleak
   - Talk that there is nothing they can do
   - Threats to harm the wife
   - Loss of interest in activities that used to give pleasure
   - Anxiety and agitation
   - Giving away things that are important to them
   - Making plans to give someone a key to the home

As research has shown, several of the above-mentioned items are also true for other age groups that commit homicide and suicide.

Box 6.1   Homicides and Suicides in Older Persons

Type   *Traits and Characteristics*

Dependent/   In this type of homicide/suicide, the couple has
Protective   been married for a long time, and they have become
                very dependent on each other. When the wife's
                health begins to fail and the husband believes he is
                no longer control of his living situation, suicide is
                seen as the answer. In another scenario, if the man's
                health is failing, he may become depressed and
                decide to kill his wife, who may or may not be ill,
                and then himself.

Caregiver/   This type of homicide/suicide is similar to the
Dependence   one mentioned above. One partner is taking care
                of the other; however, depression develops over a
                period of time. This depression is coupled with a
                sense of isolation from others and perhaps anomie.
                The only perceived choice for the male in this
                scenario is suicide.

Aggressive   In almost one in three cases, there is a history of
                spouse or partner abuse. A stressor may develop,
                such as a separation or legal action pending for
                domestic abuse, and some form of threatening
                behavior is realized or expected. This type of
                homicide/suicide occurs in older couples also.

Symbiotic   Occurring in a minority of cases (approximately
                20%), in this case, the husband and wife are both
                elderly and highly dependent on each other. Usually
                both are ill, with the male usually the stronger of the
                two with a dominant personality type.

Source: Cohen (2004).

However, when we suspect that an older couple may be destined for
such a homicide-suicide and display many or even all of the items to
look for, then immediate intervention is necessary.

A confrontation based upon concern and affection is, for many, the
first step in the intervention process. Also, know what community

resources are available. What is the telephone number of the local crisis center. Is there a suicide hotline in the community? If there is, what is the number and where is it located? The local social service agency also may have a specialist who can help.

Family Violence and Suicide Among Adolescents

In their study of adolescents in Minnesota public schools, Yexley, Borowsky, and Ireland (2002) reported that adolescents who had either witnessed or been a victim of physical violence within the family had a significantly increased risk of exhibiting physical violence themselves. Experiencing physical violence within the family is also a strong predictor of suicidal ideation.

Conclusion

The violence perpetrated against intimates is not easily understood. For some people, violence becomes a common form of human behavioral exchange, and for those who want to escape it, suicide may seem the only plausible solution to such a problem.

Notes

1. Names have been changed to protect the family's privacy.
2. Names have been changed to protect the family's privacy.

7

Suicide Letters

A Typology and Analysis

In talking with relatives of suicide victims, one of the first things they ask about is the suicide note. Most believe that if this were truly a suicide, there would be a suicide note. What we have found, quite to the contrary, is that most of the time, there are no suicide notes. In more than 100 suicides we have personally investigated, and hundreds more where we have examined the files, it appears that in only about 15% of the cases has a note been left. And as we will mention, the notes take many forms.

Suicide Notes and Letters

Investigators look for a suicide note at any potential suicide scene in order to help determine that the present scene is not an accident, a natural death, or a homicide. It is a suicide. Of course, in some rare occasions, the scene could be staged as a suicide, but this does not happen often.

The notes and letters are typically influenced by spurned love, revenge, mental illness, anger, and a multitude of other reasons. For example, see Figure 7.1. In looking at this letter, several elements are immediately visible. The writer, who shot himself in the head at his mother's home, was upset with his girlfriend, who was also the

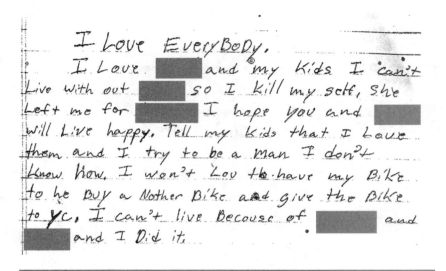

I Love EveryBoDy.
I Love ████ and my Kids I can't
Live with out ████ so I kill my self, She
Left me for ████ I hope you and ████
will Live happy. Tell my kids that I Love
them and I try to be a man I don't
know how. I won't Lou the have my Bike
to he Buy a Nother Bike and give the Bike
to yc, I can't live Becouse of ████ and
████ and I Did it.

Figure 7.1

mother of his children. To compound the problem, she had left him for a woman. He had talked with his mother before the suicide and informed her of the situation. He was apparently very emotional about his relationship with his girlfriend, and the victim's mother said that she was afraid that he was going to hurt his girlfriend, not take his own life.

We will examine other letters and notes and place them into categories for intellectual examination. We have examined more than 500 letters and notes dating from 1960 to the present. The missives have been catergorized predicated upon content, stated motivations, and other incidental contents.

Categories of Suicide
Notes and Letters

After viewing more than 500 suicide notes and letters, it is readily apparent that not all notes and letters are alike. We have identified the following categories to distinguish among the various notes and letters:

Financial, Love Scorned, Physical Health, Mental Health, and Escape From Pain.

Financial

Financial issues play a huge role in the decision to commit suicide. What may be an insurmountable obstable for one person is a trivial matter to another. One man wrote, *"I kill [sic] myself and wife,_____, tonight because the way they was [sic] doing."* The man, age 37, had received a letter from an attorney who represented a collection agency. The letter demanded $579.98 for an outstanding debt. In that man's mind, this was ample reason for him to kill his wife and then commit suicide.

In another case, a law student, age 27, was upset because he knew he would soon be arrested for embezzlement of funds from his employer. He wrote a 15-page letter to his wife, his mother, his two brothers and one sister, as well as to his employer to apologize for the problems he caused to them all. His letter admitted his own shortcomings, his lack of focus, the trouble with his financial resources, his lack of concern and affection for his wife, and other issues from which he believed there was no escape (see Figure 7.2).

Another man reported that bills and calls from collection agencies were "driving me nuts." He apologized to his wife for all the problems he caused because of his inability to provide financially for his family. He also wrote that no one understood him and how hard he had worked to make things right financially. Hopefully, one day, they would think more positively about him, but now he was just too weak to carry on any longer. He then shot himself.

In another case, a 41-year-old woman was experiencing great financial problems. A real estate salesperson, she had just been informed that she was losing her job. She tried to contact her previous employer, who would not return her calls. She had two part-time jobs selling cosmetics and educational programs, and she took chances on professional football games and other gambling endeavors. She was sinking deeper and deeper into debt.

The victim pulled her car into her garage, inserted a clothes dryer hose into the car's exhaust pipe and the other end into one of the rear

– 7 –

procrastinating trying to avoid the inevitable.

after the things came out of the Institute today about the money I've taken — I don't know how long they've been working on that but it must have been some time (no wonder they've seemed so ill at ease around me) — and after the fight you and I had this morning which was just the culmination I guess of things that have been going on for months — then my decision on what I had to do was pretty clear-cut. I could run away, but that would leave you and Teresa without any financial security + without me, too, and that is not what I want. I also don't want to be around to see this thing prolonged and to cause anybody any more pain + publicity.

Besides, as you know, the loss of my life is not all that big a thing with me any more. For the last 2½ years I have been trying to carry on 3 things — a family, a job, and law school — and through some weird talent of mine I have screwed up all three. I would say I'm just trying to do too much — but plenty of other guys are doing it + I can't see that I am inferior to them.

Figure 7.2

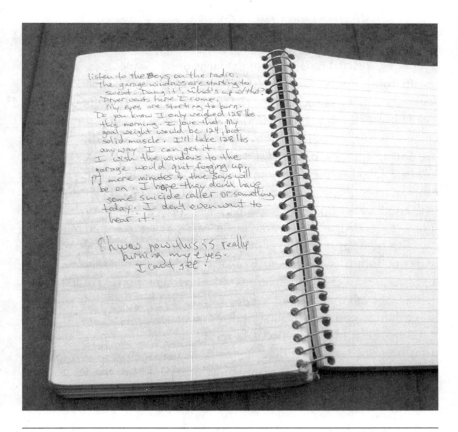

Figure 7.3   This woman stated that she was very concerned about her lack of financial stability. Her job was in jeopardy, her savings had dwindled to only a few dollars, and she was not able to meet her monthly bills. On the last of four pages, she ends with, "Oh wow, now this is really burning my eyes. I can't see."

car windows. At 10:45 a.m., she started her suicide note. Her last entry was written at 12:43 p.m. (see Figure 7.3). Further investigation by the coroner's office and the local police determined that this woman had attempted suicide on at least one other occasion in the same way, death by carbon monoxide poisoning.

What are the unique factors of financially related suicide notes? Typically, there are references to gross financial difficulties. An inability to pay off debts is commonly mentioned. Sometimes, the debts result from money loaned by family or friends; other times, business reversals or failures account for the financial plights. In addition, anticipated loss of a job because of poor performance, business downsizing, embezzlement, or other job-related problems and concerns are often present. In the case of the real estate agent, the woman was going to lose her job; her previous employer would not return her calls; her other, part-time jobs did not provide the money she needed to survive (she also had her home up for sale because of her inability to make her house payments); and with no remedies in sight, she resorted to suicide.

This case appears to be a form of fatalistic suicide coupled with elements of anomic suicide. This woman's life had changed dramatically, and previous rules and regulations were no longer present (anomic elements). She felt that she had no way to escape this unbearable situation other than to commit suicide (fatalistic element).

Regardless of the intellectual typing, those in dire financial conditions often believe that suicide is the only answer. Such action leaves the family forever wondering if something could have been done to help fix the problems. Family members are the collateral victims of suicide.

Love Scorned

Early in a new love relationship, there is a feeling that among all the people in the world, your lover has selected you. When a relationship is terminated, one person has been "deselected." Now you are not the one and only; you are now the one pushed aside for another or for another purpose.

In suicide notes that depict love scorned, there is a great deal of personal pain mentioned as well as direct words of anger, hostility, and other negative emotions toward the person once loved. This is illustrated well by the note left by "Elizabeth" in Figure 7.4.

But these emotions are not unique and occur frequently in letters. The victim also partially blames the other person or him- or herself for the "deselection process." Witness the following case.

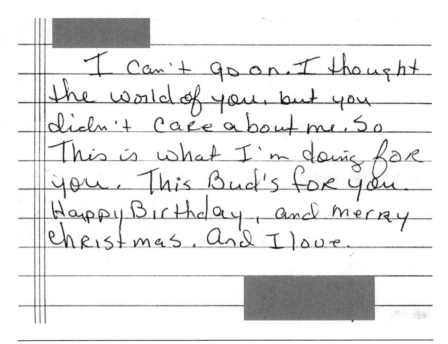

I Can't go on. I thought the world of you, but you didn't care about me. So This is what I'm doing for you. This Bud's for you. Happy Birthday, and merry christmas. and I love.

Figure 7.4   The author of this note was scorned by her ex-boyfriend. She wrote notes to her parents and sister, and this note to her ex-boyfriend. She believed that she could not go on without him. But her final written words were direct indicators of the hurt he had caused her.

A couple had been married for 10 years. He and his wife had experienced discord within their marriage, and she left him for another man. He left the following suicide note.

Dear _____,

I have never loved anyone like you. The things were [sic] done together were beautiful. I have ruined my life but not yours. You have a future and a desire. Just remember if you ever marry again, you get someone to love you as much as I did. I can only blame myself for what happened. Life is to [sic] short to live alone. I cannot live and let you suffer. I have made a fool of myself for asking you to give up your life for me.

> *Please forgive me for what I am going to do. You have a great life. I cannot give you what you deserve.*
>
> _____

In another case, a young woman wrote in her suicide note,

> *Dear _____,*
>
> *This is the only way I can have you is in my soul. I love you with all my heart. I can't share you with no one. I don't want to die, but I just want you with my only.*
>
> *Bye forever,*
>
> _____

Spurned-lover suicide notes are typically messages of an anticipated aloneness that can be remedied only through suicide. In the missives we have examined, it is apparent that in the overwhelming number of cases, the victim has been deselected by a former lover and intimate. A rekindling of the relationship is not possible, and there is no hope of a reconciliation. In a few notes, the victim states that, through his or her suicide, the other person will have a better life. Because the suicide victim considers him- or herself to be a huge part of the problem, the only way for the other person to regain hope and joy in his or her life is for the victim to permanently remove him- or herself from the other person's life. The notes typically include a sense of hopelessness about rekindling of relationship, and that all is lost.

Physical Health

When someone has a terminal illness, the main reason he or she commits suicide is to escape the pain of the illness (see Figure 7.5). The pain has been present for such a long period of time, and there is

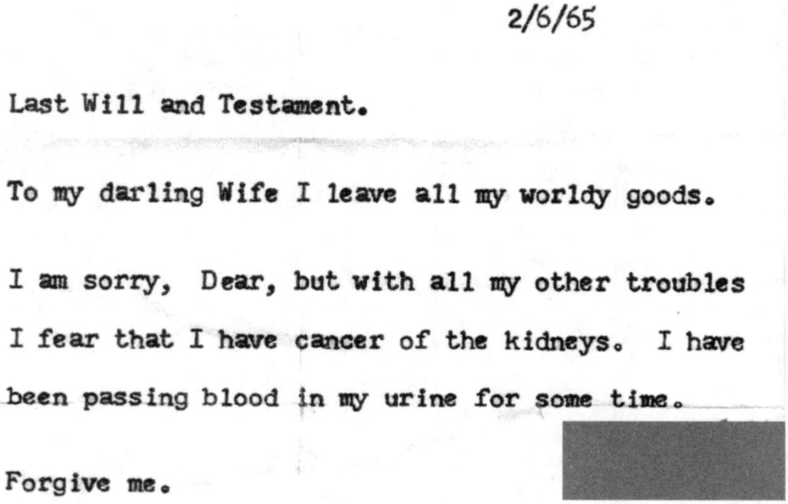

2/6/65

Last Will and Testament.

To my darling Wife I leave all my worldy goods.

I am sorry, Dear, but with all my other troubles
I fear that I have cancer of the kidneys. I have
been passing blood in my urine for some time.

Forgive me.

Figure 7.5   A businessman had not been diagnosed with cancer or any disease, but he believed he had the disease. He shot himself with his own weapon. He did not have cancer.

almost a sense of relief that a decision has been made—not necessarily to commit suicide, but that he or she will finally be free of the pain. This was evident in the suicide note left by a 76-year-old woman who simply was not willing to endure the pain any longer.

> *Dear _____,*
>
> *I am tired of the pain. I have suffered too long and yearn only for peace. It is not your fault, it is my decision.*
>
> *_____*

This same message was delivered many times over in our analysis of suicide notes, and it seems especially prevalent in the elderly.

"My wife, _____, is the most loveing [sic] careing [sic], church lady and so many more thing [sic]. She was just great, a super laday [sic]. Many men could only dream of having someone like her.

I have not had a drink since July 7, 1985. I only try [sic] this whiskey drink to help me get through all this stuff and get the nerve up to do this. I sure try to do right, but with the back pain and leg pain and other problems it was getting to me. There is so many thing [sic] I want to do, but scare [sic] to try them, that hurt [sic] me.

My wonderful wife always doing everything to keep my spirit up, she just grate [sic], like say's [sic] all love. But I feel use less [sic].

My dear _____, I will see you in Heven [sic].

Love,

_____

According to the coroner's investigative report,

This man had a long problem with back and leg pain, a result of a sciatic problem. He was advised to have a colonoscopy due to suspected cancer-like symptoms. He took a .22 caliber rifle into his bathroom while his wife was out shopping and shot himself two times in his left chest with the rifle. He fell from the commode and wedged himself against the door, causing police and EMS personnel to force open the bathroom door. The victim was dead at the scene.

This is a fatalistic suicide—the circumstances are perceived as negative, perhaps painful, and from which there was no escape. This man had mentioned to his wife that he believed he had colon cancer because his blood test results indicated a PSA reading of 12, which is high and perhaps indicative of colorectal cancer. With his leg and back problems, and now the possibility of cancer, and despite his supportive and loving partner, this latest physical challenge was too much for him to bear.

Another message we have found in suicide notes is concern for the survivors. Many letters and notes are quick to point out that the suicide is not anyone's fault. The victim made the decision with forethought and care, and the survivors should not feel any sense of culpability. The victim needed to relieve his or her pain and suffering, and he or she did not want to be a burden on his or her family.

> Dear _____ and Family,
>
> After a lot of thinking I don't want to be a burden to you. I have had a good life for many years. I hope this is not too much of a shock. Please do not worry, things will come out OK.
>
> Love,
>
> _____

Victims are constantly concerned with not being a burden to their family or caretakers. They often mention that financial resources are low, and that if the illness or injury continues, their financial reserves will be completely depleted and they will become a burden on the family. This is unacceptable to them, and so they choose death.

Mental Health

Some individuals are in such depths of depression and mental illness that they feel that committing suicide is the only way out of their deplorable condition. Other victims are psychotic and out of touch with reality.

Linda, age 46, a single white female, had a history of mental illness. Linda's mother last spoke to her the day before she committed suicide. Her mother said that Linda had not shown up for her previous three appointments with her social worker and therapist. Linda told her mother that she had forgotten, and then said she was tired and did not feel like going to the clinic for her session. Her mother reported to the deputy coroner that Linda had a history of bipolar disorder, depression, and hypertension. Linda had also attempted suicide by drug overdose about 5 years before.

After numerous attempts to contact her, several family members went to Linda's home and found her dead on the bedroom floor. She left two suicide notes. The first one read:

> I want Tommy Lee to have my car.
> I want Candy to go to the lovebirds.
> I want Mary Beth to take Baby to the vet and have her cremated.
> I want her ashes to be buried with me. She's my heart.
> Anything anybody wants, take.

Her second note was more personal and had a message of fatalism and personal pain:

> Sick of people—no one's real
> Sick of trying—what's the point
> Sick of talking—no one listens
> Sick of listening—it's all lies
> Sick of thinking—just end up confused
> Sick of moving—never get anywhere
> Sick of myself—don't want to live
> Sick and tired—and no one cares

Her family found her lying on her back and her blouse pulled up about her breasts. There was an empty prescription bottle on the floor next to her body. There were no signs of trauma and no foul play was suspected.

In another case, a woman, age 74, had been seeing a counselor for the past 10 years for depression. She had lost two children and was living with her husband, who had terminal cancer. Life was a trial every day, according to the conversations she had with her sister and two brothers. She never mentioned her feelings of depression to her husband because of her love for him. As is common with this type of suicide, she was concerned for the survivors, hoping that they would understand and forgive what she was about to do (see Figure 7.6).

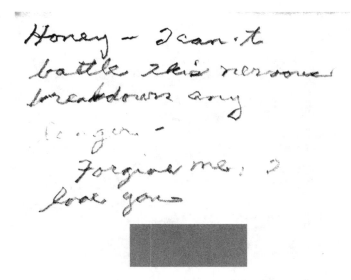

Figure 7.6   After writing this note, the woman took an overdose of her medications that included prescriptions for depression, high blood pressure, heart problems, Type II diabetes, and arthritis.

In another example, Carol, a 25-year-old single female, wrote in her suicide note about how she was "called" by Jesus and spoken to by Jesus and Job (Figure 7.7).

In some letters and notes, suicide victims who are psychotic mention voices and visions that command their behaviors and reactions, and even command that they take their own lives. Their minds have been damaged in some fashion and do not operate well in a social and/or behavioral context.

Of course, the psychotic person is not always out of touch with reality. The person may go along for days, weeks, or even months exhibiting mental well-being. Then, because of a particular situation, or physiology, or biology, or a combination of these elements, the person goes into a psychotic episode for a period of time. During that time, depression or other aspects of a mental disorder may become so pervasive that suicide seems like a viable choice to make.

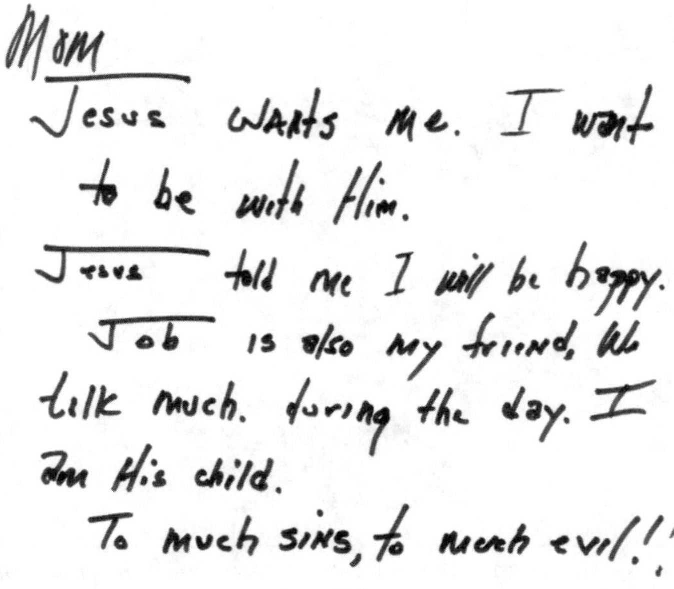

Mom

Jesus wants me. I want
to be with Him.
Jesus told me I will be happy.
Job is also my friend, We
talk much. during the day. I
am His child.
To much sins, to much evil!!

Figure 7.7   Carol had undergone hospitalization and psychiatric treatment for psychotic episodes since she was a teenager. She claimed to talk with Jesus and the Old Testament character, Job. She believed in her audio hallucinations that the religious figures were calling her to Heaven.

Often, the victim feels very alone. Consider the note left by a 17-year-old who was incarcerated in a juvenile institution. He remarked that no one understood his feelings. He was alone, lonely, and apparently without a friend with whom he could talk and from whom he could receive some type of approval. He said in his note,

> You say I am a girl-chaser. First I would like to get you on the right path. I don't chase girls, I only look at them. I guess I look too much. Why I look is because I cannot get too close to them before they head for the hills when they see me.

In another case (see Figure 7.8), a teen left a note wondering why no one had paid attention.

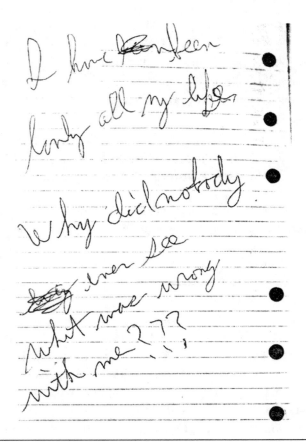

Figure 7.8   A teenager was in a depressed state because of his perceived lack of attention from his parents and his rejection by his girlfriend. He shot himself after writing this note.

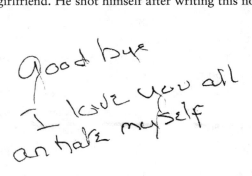

Figure 7.9   This woman was depressed. She had been in therapy for more than 5 years, but her state of self-hatred had not been resolved.

These notes often have a plea for help and forgiveness, as well as, in at least a few cases, a sense of self-loathing. This is evident in the note left by a 45-year-old wife who shot herself (see Figure 7.9). In this note, the message is clear and concise. Despite her positive feelings for others, she felt very negatively about herself.

Implications of Suicide
Notes for Suicide Investigations

A suicide note certainly has a direct connection with the investigation of a suspected suicide. The note will verify the suicide in most cases unless there are extreme circumstances. But obviously there are other lessons to be learned.

Conclusion

A suicide note often states the reasons for the suicide. For example, a note may testify to the physical health of the person. A terminal illness—one that the victim's family knew about beforehand or only learned of because of the contents of the note—is for many an understandable reason for suicide. Other stated reasons in the notes or letters can provide the survivors with a sense of understanding and acceptance.

The multitude of reasons for suicide can have important implications for those in the mental health profession involved in the research and study of suicide. Knowing the most common reasons will help not only in the investigation of suicide but also in the growing understanding of those who commit suicide.

In collecting research for this chapter and working with local detectives on violent crimes, we have developed close working relationships with the death investigators. Many of the homicide detectives are relatively new to this squad. One of the first items of physical evidence they search for is a suicide note. Now knowing that suicide notes can come in the form of traditional notes, writings on walls or mirrors, tapes, videos, and so on, they have a better idea of what to look for. They also know that in only in a minority of cases are suicide notes and letters left, perhaps as few as 20%. In the past, detectives thought that if a suicide note was not present, then the death was not a suicide; now, however, detectives know that notes are the exception rather than the rule. This is important to know in the course of suicide investigation.

8

Selected Atypical Suicides

Dr. Jack Kevorkian first helped people to commit suicide in 1990. His actions have been so dramatized that he is synonymous with physician-assisted suicides. On June 4, 1990, Kevorkian was first present at the death of a 54-year-old woman suffering from Alzheimer's disease. Using spare parts he secured from yard sales and other places, Kevorkian built a Thanatron, or "death machine." He started the process with an intravenous drip of saline solution. Then, the woman pressed a device that stopped the saline solution and started releasing thiopental on a timer, resulting in a deep coma. Finally, the timer released a lethal dose of potassium chloride, which stopped her heart.

This was not Kevorkian's only assisted suicide. Finally, in 1999, he was convicted of second-degree murder as well as the delivery of a controlled substance. He received a sentence of 10–25 years in prison with eligibility for parole after 6 years.

So, exactly what is assisted suicide? There are several types:

- *Passive Euthanasia*: quickening the death of a person by altering some form of life-support system. Examples include stopping medicines, not delivering emergency acts such as CPR, removing life support equipment, and stopping food and water.
- *Active Euthanasia*: causing the death of a person at that person's request.
- *Involuntary Euthanasia*: aiding in the death of someone who cannot make his or her own decision because he or she is in a

vegetative state or a coma. The medical team and the family firmly believe that the person will never regain consciousness.

- *Physician-Assisted Suicide*: supplying information or the means to commit suicide. This may include the physician prescribing a lethal amount of medication and some other form of death-inducing means.

Physician-Assisted Suicide

Among the very severely ill or terminally ill, while in a state of great pain, some of them may decide to commit suicide with the aid of a physician. However, when the pain passes or lessens, might they change their mind about suicide? This is an issue that demands further attention. But what is known is that physicians need additional training to evaluate when assisted suicide may be an alternative in jurisdictions where physician-assisted suicide is legal. Tulsky (2000) recommends that, while abiding by the ethics of the situation, physicians should fully disclose the total situation to their patients. They should not encourage their patients to take their own lives but rather help them to identify solutions.

Bascom and Tolle (2002) pointed out that in their study of dying patients, about half of the patients reported that they would like to have an option of physician-assisted suicide. Additionally, as a person comes

---

Box 8.1   Physician-Assisted Suicide

In a survey administered to 228 physicians studying physician-assisted suicide to HIV patients, physician-assisted suicide was defined as "a physician providing a sufficient dose of narcotics to enable the patient to kill himself."

Are there other definitions?

Source: Slome, Mitchell, Charlebois, Benevedes, and Abrams (1997).

closer to the reality of suicide, this percentage decreases. Regardless, they argue, despite the physician's personal morals and personal concerns, and without neglecting his or her own legal responsibilities, the physician's concerns should not override his or her willingness to try to understand the basic motivation of those with suicidal ideations.

Oregon became the first state to legalize assisted suicide. Slightly more than 50% of voters voiced their approval under certain conditions. In the case of someone who is seeking medication to end his or her life, the request must be in writing and witnessed by two people. The request is then sent to the patient's primary care physician. The physician must then inform the person of his or her diagnosis and prognosis, the probable result of the medication, and any feasible alternatives. The physician must get a second opinion from another physician and refer the patient for counseling if needed. Finally, there is a 15-day waiting period between the patient's request in writing and receipt of the drugs (Gesensway, 1995).

From an examination of Table 8.1, it is apparent that an overwhelming number of states are not in favor of legalizing physician-assisted suicides. This does not reflect the number of citizens who are in favor of such a law. For example, a 1999 Gallup Poll asked the question, "When a person has a disease that cannot be cured and is living in severe pain, do you think doctors should be allowed by law to assist the patient to commit suicide if the patient requests it, or not?" Sixty-one percent were in favor and 35% were opposed (Gallup Poll, 1999).

The U.S. Supreme Court has said that there is no constitutional right to physician-assisted suicide. States are free to ban it, and they are also free to permit it (Doerflinger, 1999; Vacco v. Quill, 1997). But it appears that state laws do not reflect the attitudes and values of the citizens (Snyder & Caplan, 2000).

Of course, obvious questions and issues are involved in legislating laws concerning physician-assisted suicide. First, what goals are the guidelines intended to serve? Who should formulate such guidelines for assisted suicides? What obstacles currently circumvent the successful legislation of assisted suicides? Other questions, both pro and con, can help address the issue (Caplan, Snyder, & Faber-Langendoen, 2000).

Table 8.1   Summary of Legal Status of Assisted Suicides in the United States

Thirty-seven states have laws that prohibit assisted suicide:

Alaska	Maryland	Vermont
Arizona	Michigan	West Virginia
Arkansas	Minnesota	
California	Montana	*Legal status of assisted suicide is undetermined in the following states*
Colorado	Nebraska	
Connecticut	New Hampshire	
Delaware	New Jersey	
Florida	New Mexico	District of Columbia
Georgia		Hawaii
Illinois	*Seven states prohibit assisted suicide by common law*	Nevada
Indiana		Utah
Iowa	Alabama	Wyoming
Kansas	Idaho	*One state allows assisted suicide under certain circumstances*
Kentucky	Massachusetts	
Louisiana	North Carolina	
Maine	Ohio	Oregon

Source: Americans United for Life (2001).

But should assisted suicide be the sole domain of the physician? Faber-Langendoen and Karlawish (2000) argued that physician-assisted suicide should be expanded to include a team model approach. For example, they argued that the physician's education and training do not prepare him or her adequately for this task. Other professionals, such as social workers, nurses, and the clergy, should be intimately involved.

Who Are the Patients in Physician-Assisted Suicides?

In examining the traits and characteristics of those who die in physician-assisted suicides, we recognize that the findings are limited to the study

---

Box 8.2   Legal Arguments
Concerning Physician-Assisted Suicide

Con

Usually the arguments against assisted suicide by physicians and other medical caretakers center around the possibility of a lawsuit against the medical provider. This is typically a concern when there is the possibility of a misdiagnosis of an illness or disease and the person's life was terminated by suicide with the aid of the medical caretaker.

Pro

This position is that it is better to aid the suffering or terminally ill patient, and the medical caretaker is in the best position to be of humane service. By allowing the medical caretaker to be an integral part of the suicide scenario, safeguards could be developed to aid the patient in a humane and nonpainful procedure to end his or her life with dignity and respect.

---

of only those people who are known to have died by this method. Recognizing the limitations of academic research, any finding must be viewed with some skepticism. For example, Chin, Hedberg, Higginson, and Fleming (1999) reported that of the 15 people who died in Oregon, all were white and about half (8) were male. Their median age was 69. Four of the patients had had psychiatric consultations in accordance with the state law. The researchers also pointed out that the patients who were single or divorced were more likely to die in this scenario than those who were married or widowed. But probably the most interesting finding was that the decision to commit physician-assisted suicide was more often based on the patient's concern over loss of autonomy and personal control, not on fear or pain. So, despite the common perception that those involved in physician-assisted suicide are ending their lives because of pain and suffering, the reality is more often the perceived lack of personal control over their own destinies.

More research is needed on the issues, concerns, and practice of physician-assisted suicide. Is there a place in our society for this form of suicide? If so, what should be the guidelines for implementation and practice? How should the decision be reached, and who needs to be involved? These and other questions need to be researched and debated.

Cults and Mass Suicide

In this chapter, we discuss two examples of cults and suicide. The first is Jim Jones and Jonestown, and the second is the more recent case of the Heaven's Gate cult.

Case Study: Jonestown, Guyana

Almost 1,000 people committed suicide on November 18, 1978, in Jonestown, Guyana. The Reverend Jim Jones ordered more than 900 members of his religious cult to kill themselves. Most drank a poisoned children's drink, some were shot, and others were stabbed. Jones suffered a fatal shot to his head. It was never determined if he shot himself or if he ordered someone else to kill him. Was it suicide or assisted suicide? The world was shocked by the enormity of the numbers, the atrocity surrounding the deaths, and the tragedy that occurred in the dense jungle of Guyana. What had happened, and who was responsible?

Jim Jones was born in Lynn, Indiana, in 1931. As he grew into a young man, he became interested not only in religion but also in the suffering of the downtrodden. He was ordained a minister in Indianapolis, and in 1963, he founded the People's Temple Full Gospel Church. He worked tirelessly for anyone who needed his help. He preached for racial and sexual equality and finding jobs for the unemployed, and he aided those who were in trouble.

But there were strange happenings, too. Things were not all well in Indiana. Jones was known to have fainting spells and complained of poor health. He spoke of communicating with extraterrestrials, practiced faith healing, and often predicted the imminent end of the world. Bad things were going to happen if "Father" (the name that Jones insisted his followers call him) did not intervene. One major danger was the Soviet Union. He was convinced that the Soviet Union would initiate a major bombing effort that would destroy the United States.

Because Indiana was in the Midwest and would be a certain target of a nuclear holocaust, Jones was determined to lead his flock to safer ground. He fled to Brazil, where he lived a simple life. Some believe that at that time, he was working as an agent for the Central Intelligence Agency, something that Jones never denied.

After a short time in South America, Jones returned to the United States soon after President John F. Kennedy was assassinated in 1963. Locating in San Francisco, Jones and his small band of followers became increasingly active in fundraising.

From all outward appearances, Father Jones was a loving pastor. But some former members said that he demanded absolute loyalty and obedience to his rules. Once people became full members, they gave all their financial and worldly goods to Jones. They surrendered their identification cards, Social Security cards, insurance policies, bank cards, stocks, savings accounts, and so on.

More firmly enmeshed in a schizophrenic world, Jones called himself Jesus and Lord, convincing many the end of the world was near. Now the United States was the enemy, and only Jones had an effective plan for everyone's survival and salvation. Only the members of the People's Temple would survive the impending holocaust. Jones moved the People's Temple to the jungle in Guyana and established Jonestown, which he hoped would be a self-sufficient agricultural community.

But as troubles grew, the members sent messages about conditions at Jonestown. Family members who were not part of the People's Temple grew worried about what they were hearing from their loved ones. Finally, in November 1978, Congressman Leo Ryan and a small party arrived at the encampment to investigate the allegations of mistreatment. When Ryan and his party talked with many members, most were complimentary of the manner in which they were treated and their relationship with Jones. However, two families wanted to leave with the congressman. As they gathered on the airstrip to leave, they were ambushed and fired upon by Temple gunmen. Five people, including Ryan, were killed.

Jones had told his followers prior to the shooting that Ryan and his party would be killed, and this would bring federal agents down on the group. They would all be killed. The only way to escape would be to commit suicide alongside "Father." Jones and his inner circle encouraged all of the members to drink a poisoned drink; those who refused were forced at gunpoint to drink the poison, or else they were shot. Jones was apparently one of the last to die, from a bullet to his head.

Can this be mass suicide? We believe that it can. Through Jones's persona and charisma, he was responsible for the deaths of more than 900 innocents. But was it simply his personality, charm, and charisma that accounted for his ability to lead hundreds of people to their deaths? What was it exactly that made him so successful? Certainly, the time had to be right for his message and charm to work. In the same way that Charles Manson was successful at leading his "flower children" into his own cult and doing his wishes without questions or dissension, Jones had his own unique qualities working for him. What were they?

In 1971, Stanford psychologists Philip Zimbardo and Craig Haney conducted a now-famous study that has echoes in the recent mistreatment of Iraqi prisoners by members of the U.S. military. In their study, Zimbardo and Haney asked psychology graduate students to take on the roles of guards and inmates. The "guards" adapted to their role quickly and successfully, and they became emotionally and verbally abusive toward the "inmates." The "inmates" behaved the same way toward the "guards." Did the same thing happen in Iraq? It appears so, at least to a great degree. But what about Jim Jones?

Zimbardo (1997) argued that tragedies like Jonestown can happen when rules of influence are abused by leaders of a group or cult. He noted that Jones read George Orwell's book *1984* and applied Orwell's mind control techniques to his followers, which gave them little choice other than to take their own lives. Zimbardo lists four mind control methods that Jones used.

Big Brother Is Watching You

Jones demanded that his underlings spy on each other to ensure that his rules and principles were being followed at all times. He also made sure that his personal, dogmatic, and intrusive messages were heard constantly via loudspeakers across the encampment. Regardless of where one wandered, intentionally or not, one could not escape Jim Jones's doctrine and domination.

Self-Incrimination

The members of the Jonestown cult were instructed to tell the inner circle members, and Jones himself, of any personal transgressions. They were also told to inform those in authority of any fears or doubts they may have about the cult or the leaders, including Jones. They were also instructed that these comments would not be used against them; it was all for their own good, and everlasting life in Heaven would be their reward. Needless to say, their statements were later used against them, and harsh punishments were meted out for any such statements. Any members whose statements were directed against Jones were punished especially harshly.

Suicide Drills

In George Orwell's *1984,* he made a statement to the effect that the best way to deal with the enemy's capturing you, making you suffer, and eventually killing you was to commit suicide. This was preferable to being captured in war. Thus, Jim Jones had his people practice suicide drills to prepare them if the occasion ever arose where suicide would be the appropriate and ordered action.

Distorting People's Perceptions

Using Orwell's concept of "newspeak," Jones gave his followers conflicting messages. For example, Zimbardo (1997) stated that Jones offered conflicting or blurred messages about what reality was. For example, Jones demanded that his followers thank him for their food and work, but the reality of the situation was that many of his cult members were on the verge of starvation and working 6½ days a week.

Zimbardo (1997) stated that Jim Jones was clearly a master of mind control. Because of his personality and the manner in which he was able to control the minds and behavior of others, even to the point of suicide, he was probably one of the most capable people in modern history.

Case Study: The Heaven's Gate Cult

In March 1997, 39 people were found dead in a mansion outside the city of San Diego, California. The victims were members of a quasi-religious cult named Heaven's Gate. Few outsiders had heard of this group before its mass suicide, but afterward, the names of the cult and its leader, Marshall Applewhite, became household words. Who was Applewhite, and why did 39 people take their own lives? These questions, and others, are not answered easily. We perhaps shake our heads when we think of the deaths of this small group of fanatical followers of their leader. What would compel them to take their own lives?

A former member of the Heaven's Gate cult, alerted by videotaped messages he had received in the mail, went to the mansion outside San Diego and discovered the bodies of 39 cult members. He called the police, who quickly arrived at the scene. They noted that there were no signs of struggle. The 39 people—21 women and 18 men ranging in age from 20 to 72—were reposing on their beds and cots, all dressed similarly. Some had plastic bags over their faces, and all had died of a lethal mixture of alcohol and barbiturates.

Where did this all begin? In the early 1970s, Applewhite started this small cult by preaching that a large group of aliens had come to earth to study the humans who populated this planet. The aliens were not male or female in their original form. Instead, when they arrived on earth, "containers" were ready for them that resembled human form—some male and some female. Their mission was to study the earth forms and to report to those in the next world, the higher world, what earth was all about and how humans behaved. The cult always remained small in number, probably no larger than 50. The members fervently believed the gospel of Applewhite, and there were apparently few defections.

Applewhite was a charismatic leader, and was sometimes called an overachiever. He was born in 1931, the son of a Presbyterian minister in Texas. He grew up moving from one location to another as his father started new churches. Talented in music, he sang in a few operas and taught music at the University of St. Thomas in Houston. He was also a choir director at St. Mark's Episcopal Church in Houston. Married with two children, he left his family in 1972 and met Bonnie Lu Nettles. In 1975, both claimed to be space aliens and convinced 20 people to leave their homes and move to Oregon, where they would meet with a spaceship. The spaceship never arrived. Undaunted, the group moved to California and resurfaced in 1993, when they took out an advertisement in a local newspaper proclaiming that the earth would be restructured. The Heaven's Gate members were Christian-based angels sent to earth from the early 1960s to the present time.

Applewhite apparently had the charm and charisma to carry out this plan. To illustrate the full impact of his leadership, many of the men, including Applewhite, were castrated. All of the bodies had a uni-sex look. Their heads were shaved and they were dressed in baggy clothes resembling those of monks. This was perhaps the reason for the initial reports that all the victims were men.

Why would educated and intelligent people kill themselves at the insistence of their group leader? What ideal did they believe so strongly that they were willing to forfeit their lives for it? What was supposed to occur after they departed from their "containers"? The basic belief was that the members of the group committed suicide so that they could rendezvous with a UFO that was approaching earth behind the Hale-Bopp comet. By doing so, they could avoid the end of the world, which they expected to occur at the end of the 20th century. As a friend of one of the "monks" of the group said,

> "All I can tell you is that they believed that they were going to be taken away by, as odd as this sounds, I'm just telling you what I heard, by a UFO.
>
> "That a UFO would come by and pick them up. Several months ago one of the members of the group who was one of the ones that committed suicide yesterday asked me if I was aware that there was a comet that would be coming close to earth.
>
> "They explained to me that they believed that there was a UFO following behind that comet and using it as a shield so it could not be detected by earth and that the UFO may very well be the one to take them away." (Holmes & Holmes, 2001, pp. 80–84)

Terrorism

Since September 11, 2001, terrorism has become a household word. Terrorism is often accompanied by altruistic suicide, or offering one's life for a cause. The terrorists of September 11 boarded those planes and willingly committed suicide. They did it not so much to kill and maim particular people, as to cause psychological distress to their opponents and cause politicians to make policy changes that would meet the demands of the terrorists (Hoffman & McCormick, 2004).

What kind of person commits suicide in a terrorist scenario? Lester, Yang, and Lindsay (2004) reported in their study of suicide bombers that their subjects possessed the following personal and family traits:

- Feelings of hopelessness and anger
- Disturbed personal identities
- Urge for vengeance against perceived enemies
- Borderline personality disorder
- Identification with a charismatic leader
- Strong desire to be a martyr
- Submission to an authoritarian leader
- Aggression, power, and toughness
- Strict and rigid religious background

Conclusion

It may be that social contagion and interactional amplification play an integral role in suicide when certain conditions are present. In the instance of physician-assisted suicide, the feelings of losing personal control and autonomy may lead one to a decision of suicide, and the physician's presence may legitimize that decision. For many people, this may be the last subjective obstacle to overcome.

Concerning suicide and cult behavior, the presence of a Jim Jones or a Marshall Applewhite may be the leverage necessary for the life-ending decision. The promise of everlasting salvation from a leader who is considered to be a direct representative of God is difficult for the cult member to ignore or deny. The interaction between the member and the leader is paramount to the decision. As difficult as it may be to understand, it is plain and clear to the person who is a believer. Suicide becomes an affirmative behavior to a pseudo-religious command.

What can be said with certainty is that mass suicides will not end with the Heaven's Gate episode. There will be other Jonestowns and Heaven's Gates. That is a certainty, a very sad certainty.

9

Suicide Investigation

In a suicide investigation, many important physical and nonphysical items must be considered. In this chapter, we will present topics for discussion that help determine whether a case is an accident, a suicide, or a homicide.

How does one determine whether a death is a suicide? What is it about the death scene that differentiates it from a homicide or a natural death? What is the interplay between the physical and nonphysical evidence that would alert the investigator to a suicide? What are other items that should be considered? We have already mentioned some of the evidence to examine (i.e., suicide notes and letters), but we need to fully explore a death scene in order to develop a strategy for investigation and resolution.

Suicide Investigation

The determination of the manner of death—natural, accident, homicide, suicide, unknown, or still pending—is one of the most difficult tasks for a death investigator to undertake. To make such a determination, the investigator must use all of the information at hand. For example, does the death appear to be self-inflicted? There are several ways to make this determination. A postmortem examination may make this verification for the death investigator. An autopsy, statements made by family members or witnesses, or the investigative process can also help. For example, suppose the cause of death was a gunshot wound. What would the death investigator look for in such a scenario? If the fatal wound was directed at the head, there should be a contact or near-contact wound to the head. If the fatal shot was to the torso with a long gun, the wound would have a spiral in one direction or the other. For example, there should be a downward left-to-right trajectory in right-handed people and a downward right-to-left trajectory in left-handed people. With a torso shot, a contact wound is almost always present; with a head wound, the wound can be either contact or near-contact.

We turn now to a discussion of various methods of committing suicide.

Self-Inflicted Gunshot Wounds

According to Handgun-Free America (http://www.handgun.org), there are more than 200 million guns in the United States. The organization states that firearm suicide is the most deadly, with a death resulting in almost 9 out of 10 attempts. In the cases we have noted so far, handguns and rifles are especially prevalent in cases involving elderly men and women. Although many people are opposed to gun control of any type, it is true that easy access to guns will have an effect on the rise of suicides in this country among all age groups. Ludwig and Cook (2000) found that implementation of the Brady Handgun Violence Prevention Act of 1994, which established a nationwide requirement that licensed firearms dealers observe a waiting period and perform a background check on those people purchasing handguns, has not reduced overall suicide rates. It may be that the quicker and easier it is to access a gun, the quicker the suicide.

We have witnessed handguns placed at various parts of the body, but the most prevalent body positioning is the side of the head. In our study of suicides in Louisville, Kentucky, it appears that for elderly males, inside the mouth is the most preferred position. With elderly females, it is the side of the head. With both males and females at large, it is the side of the head.

Table 9.1   Guns and Suicide Rate per 100,000 people by Age

Age	Suicide Rate
10–14	.055
15–19	4.51
20–24	7.41
25–29	6.85
30–34	6.28
35–39	6.83
40–44	7.38
45–49	7.49
50–54	7.92
55–59	7.52
60–64	7.80
65–69	8.39
70–74	10.40
75–79	12.37
80–84	14.16
85–89	12.99

Source: Adapted from *The Sourcebook on Criminal Justice Statistics, 2004,* Table 3.142.

Examining the information in Table 9.1, it is apparent that as people grow older, they are more inclined to use firearms in their commission of suicide. There is a general increase in numbers until it peaks at the age cohort of 80–84 years. In the last age grouping of 85–89, there is a small decline, but it still is the second highest number. In the age group of 15–19, there is a strong increase in suicide by firearms over the cohort of 10–14, which may simply be the availability of weapons to someone who is at least 15 years old.

So, what are some of the crime scene traits that the medical examiner should look for when investigating a suspected suicide by gunshot?

Searing

Searing is burning of the skin that results from hot gases emitting from a gun barrel. It is present when the gun was in close contact with the victim's skin. The soot resulting from the gunshot will burn into the edge of the wound.

There are other factors to consider with searing, but for our purposes, suffice it to say that searing plays an integral role in the examination of a shooting to determine the distance of the gun from the victim's body.

Trace Evidence

Trace evidence on the hands may confirm that the victim was holding the weapon at the time it was discharged. Blood need not be present on the hands, even with a contact wound, and may not be present on the weapon regardless of the distance from which the shot was fired.

Position

Handguns are typically held to the temple, behind the ear, to the side or front of the forehead, in the mouth, under the chin, or even to the heart. Long guns are often fired upwards. If a long gun is used, the investigator must determine if the victim was able to reach the trigger to fire the weapon. Although that point seems obvious, it must be mentioned because it is often ignored.

Entry and Exit Wounds

The entry wound is important to consider. It may contain evidence such as soot, powder burns, an abrasion ring, and possibly bullet wipe if the bullet penetrated clothing. It is typically the approximate size of the projectile.

The exit wound is usually larger than the entry wound, except when the part of the body where the projectile exits is pressed against a hard surface. The exit wound is typically less regular in shape than the entry wound. Sometimes, if a victim had a change of mind at the last minute, there is evidence of grazes where the victim apparently moved slightly before firing a shot. Of course, by examining the grazes, the professional death investigator can determine the directionality of the activity.

Postmortem Activity of the Body

After a person has shot him- or herself, the person may or may not remain at the location where the act occurred. Gunshot victims have moved themselves long distances. Dr. Tracey Cory, medical examiner in Kentucky, has stated that a person can function for several seconds after his or her heart has stopped functioning (T. Cory, personal communication, May 10, 2004). In some cases, to illustrate the point, victims have shot themselves two times despite the first shot being fatal.

Hanging

Hanging is the second or third most popular means of suicide, depending on the area of the country. Hanging victims often leave suicide notes.

The most common knot used in a suicidal hanging is the slip knot, rather than the "hangman's knot." The knot is usually placed at the side of the neck, but having the knot at the back of the head is also effective. Placing the knot at the front of the neck is less effective but can be fatal if the full weight of the body is hanging free.

Usually, the hanging victim will have a pale face and a protruding tongue. The tongue will have dried out by the time the investigator gets there. However, if the jugular vein was closed off prior to the carotid artery being closed off, the victim will have a congested face that is puffy and red. The presence of petechiae indicates death by strangulation.

When first called to the scene of a hanging, the investigator should take pictures of the scene before cutting down the body. Diagrams and measurements should also be taken, as well as an inventory of other death scene items. If the investigator removes the cord or rope from the body, he or she should preserve the integrity of the noose. In Kentucky, for example, the medical examiner prefers the noose still attached when the body is examined, and then ships the body to the morgue with the noose still in place.

Poisons

The most common poisons used for suicide today are various dangerous medications. There are, however, many other poisons used to commit suicide.

Chemicals

When looking for a way to commit suicide, a person might often turn to chemicals that can be found in the home. Arsenic, for example, is tasteless, and one gram of the substance can kill a person in an hour. Potassium cyanide can cause the death of a person in under 15 minutes. White phosphorous can cause death either immediately or within several hours, depending on the amount ingested. Damage can affect the liver, kidneys, heart, and nervous system. Mercury can also be fatal and has been used by several people who have committed suicide in Louisville. Contrary to common belief, the metallic mercury found in thermometers is not toxic.

Iodine, barium, cadmium, sodium fluoride (in quite large doses—5 grams), ethylene glycol (often found in antifreeze), and diethylene glycol are other substances often used to cause death in a person.

Plants

Most plant poisons act as depressants on the central nervous system. Death from an overdose of any of these poisons is caused by depression of the central nervous system, which causes paralysis of the lung and heart muscles and leads to asphyxia. The victim progresses through drowsiness, delirium, convulsions, and coma before dying. The victim also will be cyanotic, like a heart attack victim.

What are some of these plant poisons? Castor beans contain ricin, and the ingestion of only one bean can easily kill a person. The toxic effect of ricin occurs from 12 to 36 hours after exposure. Precatory bean plants, which can be purchased from nurseries, have red, pea-shaped seeds that have been used in the past as rosary beads. The seeds contain a phytotoxin called abrin, and if it comes into direct contact with the skin, it causes a severe skin rash. Water hemloch needs only a small amount of exposure, 2-3 grams of the plant, to kill. Yellow oleander can cause death within 24 hours of initial ingestion. Nicotine from tobacco, as well as yew, monkshood, zigadenus, potato sprouts, woods hemlock, jimson weed, thorn apple, mandrake, henbane, belladonna, and autumn crocus are other examples of plant poisons. Their presence can be determined through careful medical and toxicology examinations.

Pills

Traditionally, the most common pills used for suicide have been tranquilizers and sleeping pills, which all affect the central nervous system. An overdose causes the heart or lungs to cease functioning, resulting in death by asphyxia.

Suicide by overdose of antidepressants is becoming more popular now with the increased medical concern over suicide. Antidepressants have a number of different formulations, and the various formulations are produced and marketed under a variety of names. All of them are prescription drugs, and many of them are highly toxic if taken in the wrong dosage.

Illegal Drugs

Although it is possible to commit suicide by an overdose of illegal drugs, it is unusual for such a death to be ruled a suicide. Many states now label it as murder and consider the drug seller to be the murderer. This is true in the majority of states in the United States.

As little as 1 gram of either heroin or morphine can kill anyone. Codeine, an opiate, is milder than morphine, but a 1-gram dosage can cause death. Cocaine can cause death with as little as 20 mg or as much as 1.4 grams, depending on the method of ingestion.

Carbon Monoxide

It takes an atmospheric concentration of four parts per thousand of carbon monoxide for an hour to kill a human being. The victim's skin typically turns cherry red or cherry pink (on a black or Hispanic

Figure 9.1   This case depicts a realtor who was in deep financial and personal ruin. She kept a large diary, writing how she wanted to die. The victim ran the piping from her clothes dryer from her muffler to the side, rear window. From her writings, it took her more than 2 hours to die.

person, this will show up under the fingernails and on the lips). The victim goes into convulsions, which may be violent enough to move the body several yards or contort it into positions that may seem hard to explain.

The investigation into an automotive carbon monoxide poisoning should always address whether the car was still running at the time the death was discovered. If the first responder finds the car not running, the investigator must account for this before concluding the investigation.

Carbon monoxide is a colorless, tasteless, nonirritating gas. Its most frequent source as a suicide tool is automobile exhaust (see Figure 9.1). It is not unusual for suicidal carbon monoxide victims to lock or even nail the garage door shut and put padding around supposed air leaks. Although it is possible for a carbon monoxide poisoning to be accidental, that circumstance is rare. Automobile exhaust contains a number of other gases mixed with carbon monoxide that are extremely irritating and cause gagging and violent coughing. It is difficult to explain how a victim could succumb to them without first becoming aware that there was a problem.

A suicide victim does not have to be in an enclosed space to commit suicide by carbon monoxide from automotive exhaust. Simply lying near the exhaust pipe and breathing the exhaust gases can cause an 80% displacement of oxygen in the blood after some time.

The death process of carbon monoxide victims frequently includes strong convulsions. This is apparently caused by the onset of brain damage early in the process. The convulsions can be strong enough to move the body across a floor or move it around within an enclosed passenger compartment. In examining the death scene, investigators should keep these convulsions in mind. For instance, two lovers found locked in an embrace in a car would not appear to be a carbon monoxide death unless they have used artificial means to restrain themselves in the embrace.

The most obvious sign of carbon monoxide poisoning is the cherry red appearance of the lips and fingernails. Livor mortis in fair-skinned people is also cherry red. The rest of the skin will have a robust, healthy appearance rather than the usual pallor of death. In addition, if the victim has been dead for some time, there may be premature skin slippage; that is, the skin will be loose on the body. This is due to the elevated temperature inside the car caused by the car's exhaust coming in the passenger compartment.

Self-Smothering

Intentional suicides by smothering usually involve a plastic bag placed over the head. To eliminate the possibility of homicide, check the hands for evidence of restraint. Look inside the lips for tooth mark impressions, where someone might have pressed the plastic against the victim's mouth. Even a moderately small amount of force will leave tooth marks inside the lips that will remain after death.

When a plastic bag is placed over the head, it is impossible for the lungs to pass oxygen. Under these conditions, it takes about 90 seconds to pass out and about 4 minutes to die. The bag need not be tied at the bottom. Even a loose bag will effectively seal off the mouth and nose.

Do not overlook the possibility that the death could have been accidental. Plastic bags are also used by paint sniffers and as a means of sex-heightening asphyxia.

Self-Inflicted Knife Wounds

When knives are used in a homicide, defense wounds are typically found on the victim's hands and forearms. They may look much worse than the fatal wounds. Defense wounds can be distinguished from suicidal hesitation marks by their depth and severity and, to a lesser extent, by their location and orientation along the body.

It is not possible to determine precisely the angle of a stab wound. Any determination of the angle should be stated as only an approximation, and this should be done by the medical examiner.

Most nonfatal self-inflicted knife wounds may be an attempt by the victim to gain attention. These wounds are relatively neat, shallow, or parallel wounds. In general, suicidal wounds are similar, only more severe. Psychotic people have occasionally cut themselves with severely painful multiple wounds; this is also true for those people who are in extreme pain because of an illness, accident, or disease.

Suicidal knife wounds are usually very superficial with hesitation marks very close by on the skin. These are caused by the knife being held poised on the skin in preparation for the actual cut or stab. They may be so close to the actual wound that they are partially obscured by the wound or the swelling around it.

Except for wrist slashing, successful suicide by self-inflicted knife wounds is rare. As with homicide, it tends to be associated with passionate incidents.

Jumping

People who commit suicide by jumping often leave notes. They may not, however, leave them in obvious places. The death investigator should check the victim's car, purse, apartment, workplace, and school locker, as appropriate. Often, the jumpers pick bridges, buildings, and other high places that have been used by others attempting suicide. Almost every community has places that have been used for this method of suicide.

Drowning

A drowning suicide may look very much like an accident. What distinguishes a drowning suicide, in addition to the usual psychological autopsy factors, is that the victim does not struggle. Witnesses, if any, may say the victim intentionally entered the water and made no attempt to escape.

A number of postmortem changes identify drowning as the cause of death. Forensically, these include the formation of edema in the mouth, nose, and airway; water in the lungs; water in the stomach; dilation of the right ventricle of the heart; a swollen brain; and, in most cases, water damage to the surface of the lungs.

The drowning victim's body typically sinks shortly after death. It will resurface 3 days to 3 weeks after death, depending on a variety of circumstances. Surfacing is caused by bloating that increases the volume of the body without increasing the weight. Sometimes, because of air trapped in the clothing on the victim, the body will not sink at all. In other cases, the body may be caught by an underwater object and not allowed to rise.

In very cold water, the putrefaction process is very slow, and the body may not bloat up, so it will not resurface for a very long time.

Pedestrian Traffic Suicides

To be struck by an oncoming car is not an uncommon means of suicide. A typical scenario is that suicide victims lie down in the middle of the road, sometimes intoxicated, and usually at night. In this case, there would not be front-end body damage to the car, and the victims will have wheel marks and usually other marks that indicate they were struck by the undercarriage of the car.

Intentional Traffic Crashes

The intentional traffic accident is probably the most common means of suicide that is typically misclassified. Unless the person has left a suicide note, it is not obvious from the physical evidence that the crash was anything other than an accident. This is especially true because it is not uncommon for such drivers to be drunk at the time of these "accidents." The typical scenario for this kind of suicide is that it looks as if the driver fell asleep at the wheel, and the investigator will find no skid marks. He or she may also find that the car has run off the road at a sharper angle than would be true for someone who has simply lost control of a moving car. This sharper angle is the result of a decisive turn of the wheel rather than just a swerve off the road. Another common aspect is that the car will have gone head first into a very solid object at an unnaturally high speed.

One means of positively demonstrating that the accident was intentional is to examine the soles of the shoes the victim was wearing and compare them with any impressions left on the brake and throttle pedals. If the victim was intentionally driving into the solid object, he or she may have continued accelerating right up to the point of impact rather than trying to slow the car by putting a foot on the brake. If the shoe has any distinctive pattern whatsoever, it may be transferred onto the brake pedal by the sudden impact. If the shoe has a flat, unpatterned sole, then the pattern of the brake pedal or throttle pedal may be impressed into the sole of the shoe. It takes some sophisticated lighting techniques to determine these patterns sometimes, but they are very solid evidence of the intent of the driver.

Head-on car-truck accidents should also be analyzed as possible suicides when it appears that the lone driver of the car was in the wrong lane and should have seen the truck coming. The presumed insurance settlement forthcoming to the car driver's family, and the spectacular nature of the death, may motivate some people to use this method.

Fire

Although not unheard of, suicide by fire is rare (Geberth, 1996, p. 367). In 2004, a 56-year-old woman, tormented by voices and demons, doused herself with a flammable liquid and set herself on fire. Apparently changing her mind, she jumped into a small pond on her property to extinguish the fire. She died several days later in the hospital (Jefferson County Coroner files).

Suicide by fire is rare, but when it happens, it is usually committed by a woman if there is no one else involved, such as the case mentioned above. However, our research also indicates that in many cases, a male will kill members of his own family, usually by a gun or rifle of some type, and then kill himself by fire. A typical case occurred in 2004 when a man set fire to his estranged wife and their three children, all under the age of 5. He then set himself on fire (Jefferson County Coroner files).

It may be that fire setting as a method of suicide is more prevalent among women than men because men typically have better access to other methods (e.g., a handgun) and are also more experienced with firearms than are women. According to Major Henry Ott of the Arson Squad of the Louisville (Kentucky) Metro Police Department, the predominant liquid used to commit suicide by fire is gasoline. However, he added, gasoline is very explosive and thus unpredictable.

Railroad Accidents

In 2004 in the coroner's office in Louisville, we have been called to two suicides. One case was a 16-year-old boy who had just broken up with his 15-year-old girlfriend. Walking home from his part-time job in the fast food industry, the young boy walked on the railroad track. An oncoming train blew its whistle as a warning. The youngster turned his head, acknowledging the train—as reported by witnesses—and stopped with his back to the train. The train ran over him.

In another case, a 14-year-old boy had an argument with his mother. He walked a block to the railroad track, lay across the rails, and waited until the oncoming train ran over him. Three witnesses testified that they ran to try to pull the boy from the tracks but that they were too late.

In neither case was there a suicide note, but there was no mistake in recognizing the act of suicide. We have had five other cases in the past year where someone was killed in a crossing lane by a train. In each case, the car was stopped, straddling the tracks. In each case, there was no note.

The death investigator should probe the victim's background, looking for suicide notes and letters and any other personal communications with significant others, friends, and relatives.

Conclusion

In the investigation of suicide, the alert death investigator must be aware of what to look for because sometimes the circumstances of the death may confuse its classification as a suicide, a natural death, an accident, or a homicide.

In this chapter, we have looked at various methods of suicide, such as poisoning and drug overdoses. The death investigator must be aware of the characteristics of each type of death. There must also be a special sensitivity toward the family of the deceased. Many times, they are aware of the victim's propensity to commit suicide from previous attempts, but sometimes the deceased succeeds on the first try. Nonetheless, the survivors deserve some care and consideration.

10

Depression, Drugs, Alcohol, and Suicide

In this book, we have stressed environmental problems and issues that influence behavior, including suicide. Depression and the use and abuse of drugs and alcohol, all of which we will cover in this chapter, also influence suicidal behavior. Are these relationships direct or spurious? Are certain types of drugs used more frequently in the commission of suicide? What exactly is the role of alcohol in suicide? These and other questions will be addressed in this chapter.

Suicide: The Role of Depression, Alcohol, and Drugs

In our work in the coroner's office, we have noted that in many cases of suicide, some form of alcohol or drugs is present. The alcohol is typically beer or hard liquor. The drugs we have found at suicide scenes include oxycodone hydrochloride, or oxycontin; crack cocaine; and marijuana. But what role does depression play?

Depression and Suicide

What are some of the signs of depression? Moodiness, feelings of guilt, a sense of pessimism, anger, sadness, and lack of energy may be seen in a person by some members of the family and other social peers.

In addition, many people exhibit irritability, poor appetite, lack of success on the job or in school, and a tendency to engage in social activities that are self-destructive and unproductive (Goldstein & Goldstein, 1992).

What is the relationship between depression and suicide? Kempton and Forehand (1992) report that depression should be a high-level indicator of potential suicide. In their study, they found that depression plays such an important role that mental health professionals should pay as much attention to depression as they do to other risk factors. This appears to be more true for the white female population than for males and other racial groups. Lewinsohn, Rohde, Seeley, Klein, and Gotlib (2000) reported that a history of family depression also should be considered as a strong risk factor for suicide. If a person not only is depressed but also has a strong antisocial personality as well as a borderline personality issue, this person should be considered a very high risk for suicide. Weissman et al. (1999) suggested that depression is more debilitating when it arises during adolescence than when it occurs in an older person. This point of view is also shared by Merikangas, Wicki, and Angst (1994), who added that the repetitive and recurrent episodes of depression have an especially strong influence on suicide.

Sheras (2000) tells us that depression, accompanied by the abuse of alcohol and drugs, is one of the most common diagnostic formulations to describe a youth bent on self-destruction. Sheras says that the death rate among youth is almost five times as great when there has been a diagnosis of depression and certain conduct disorders, accompanied by drug use. Studies also indicate that the risk of suicide in alcoholics is 50% to 70% greater than in the general population. Studies show that individuals suffering from a major affective disorder have a suicide rate that is more than 50% higher than the rate for the general population. Lifetime risk for suicide in the general population is 1%, compared with 15% for people suffering from depression and 15% for alcoholics. Studies of alcoholics reveal that between 30% and 60% suffer from depression, and a significant proportion of alcoholics have other family members who suffer from depression.

Stressful life events can also have a major impact on someone who is already depressed. Adams, Overholser, and Spirito (1996) reported that "exit events" (e.g., death, divorce, separation) are significant events that may have a profound effect on a person and hasten or even initiate suicidal ideation. In addition, this effect may be more prevalent in women and girls than in men and boys. Groholt, Ekeberg, Wichstrom, and Haldorsen (2000) added that lack of support from family members and low socioeconomic status also play a role.

So, from this current perspective, before we consider the influence of drugs and alcohol, we have to consider many other social and psychological items that contribute to depression (Klerman, 1986; Patros & Shamoo, 1989). Straus and Kantor (1991) reported that other family issues, such as excessive physical abuse and spousal abuse, also are strong contributing factors.

So what does this say? It suggests strongly that there is a direct relationship between depression and suicide as well as alcoholism and suicide (Loucks, 1998; Porsteinsson et al., 1997; Spirito, Mehlenbeck, Barnett, Lewander, & Voss, 2003). Is the relationship between drugs and suicide as strong? This is the focus of the next section of this chapter.

Box 10.1   Standard Signs of Depression

- Persistent sad, anxious, or "empty" moods
- Feelings of anomie
- Feelings of guilt and worthlessness
- Loss of interest in previously pleasurable activities
- Decreased energy
- Change in appetite or fatigue
- Difficulty concentrating
- Thoughts of suicide
- Persistent complaining of "not feeling well"

Source: National Institute of Mental Health. Available: http://www.nimh.nih.gov/healthinformation/depressionmenu.cfm

Drugs and Suicide

With some high-risk juveniles, drug overdose is a common means of suicide (Sabatino & Smith, 1990). This is especially true for females who abuse marijuana (Kinkel, Bailey, & Josef, 1989). In the study of risk factors for suicide, a great deal of the research has centered around poor school performance, psychological distress, and sexual paraphilias, but more recent research has indicated that other risk factors need to be examined (Mahowald, Schenck, Goldner, Bachelder, & Cramer-Bornemann, 2003; Soloff, Lynch, Kelly, Malone, & Mann, 2000). For example, Bolognini, Plancherel, Laget, and Halfon (2003) reported that dysfunctional families contribute to an adolescent's suicidal tendency. They added that when there is family dysfunction, other negative experiences are more apt to follow, including drug abuse, alcoholism, and suicide. It may be that experiences with alcohol and drugs are a form of slow suicide (Downey, 1991).

Cocaine is often found in suicide scenes. Cocaine typically takes one of two forms, the white crystalline powder or "crack," which is the freebase form of cocaine and gets its name from the crackling sound that occurs when heating the sodium bicarbonate (baking soda) or ammonia used during production. Powder cocaine is usually snorted or dissolved in water and injected. Crack is most often smoked. Crack cocaine's effects can be felt almost immediately after smoking and can last from a few minutes to more than 10 minutes. The effects of snorting cocaine can last from 15 to 30 minutes and give a more intense high. The Drug Policy Information Clearinghouse stated that there are more than 2,707,000 chronic users of cocaine and slightly more than 3 million occasional cocaine users in the United States (Office of National Drug Control Policy, 2003).

From the information in Table 10.1, it is apparent that powder cocaine use grows higher as the age cohort rises. That is, the 26-and-older cohort has the higher reported use of cocaine. From the information we have gathered in our own suicide cases, we have not found cocaine in any suicide case of a person under the age of 15. On the

Table 10.1   Percentage of Americans Reporting Lifetime Use of Cocaine, by Age Group, 2002

Age Group	Lifetime	Past Year	Past Month
12–17	2.7	2.1	0.6
18–25	15.4	6.7	2.0
26 and older	15.9	1.8	0.7
Total population	14.4	2.5	0.9

Source: National Survey on Drug Use and Health. Available: http://www.oas.samhsa.gov/nhsda/2k3nsduh/2k3Results.htm

other hand, we have found cocaine at the death scenes of adults who committed suicide. All were over the age of 30.

To Get a High?

Snorting—15–30 minutes
Smoking—5–10 minutes

Although crack is not used as frequently as powder cocaine, its use follows the same trend as powder cocaine (see Table 10.2). Thus, the older the age cohort, the more likely crack will be involved. We have found that to be true in our own cases.

Table 10.2   Percentage of Americans Reporting Lifetime Use of Crack, by Age Group, 2002

Age Group	Lifetime	Past Year	Past Month
12–17	0.7	0.4	0.1
18–25	3.8	0.9	0.2
26 and older	3.9	0.7	0.3
Total population	3.6	0.7	0.2

Source: National Survey on Drug Use and Health. Available: http://www.oas.samhsa.gov/nhsda/2k3nsduh/2k3Results.htm

Box 10.2   Street Terms for Cocaine

All-American drug	Icing
Aspirin (powder cocaine)	Jelly
Barbs	Lady
Basa (crack cocaine)	Mama coca
Base (crack cocaine)	Mojo
Bernie	Nose stuff
Big C	Oyster stew
Black rock (crack cocaine)	Paradise
CDs (crack cocaine)	Pariba (powder cocaine)
Candy sugar (powder cocaine)	Pearl
Coca	Real tops (crack cocaine)
Crack	Rocks (crack cocaine)
Double bubble	Roxanne (crack cocaine)
Electric Kool-Aid (crack cocaine)	Scorpion
Flave (powder cocaine)	Sevenup
Florida snow	Snow White
Foo foo	Sugar boogers
Gin	Twinkie (crack cocaine)
Gold dust	Yam (crack cocaine)
Happy dust	Zip

Source: Office of National Drug Control Policy. Available: http://www. whitehousedrugpolicy.gov/streetterms/ByType.asp?intTypeID=3

Regardless, in adults, the use of alcohol and drugs as connected to suicide occurance does not seem to be as pronounced as in adolescents. Langevin, Paitich, Orchard, Handy, and Russon (1982), in their classic study, stated that the use of intoxicants plays a very important role in the commission of violent crimes, including suicide attempts (see Figure 10.1).

Dealing with the drug issue, drugs are seen as a major influence on adolescent suicide behavior (Laws & Turner, 1993). This is especially true when an adolescent commits suicide with a firearm. Combined

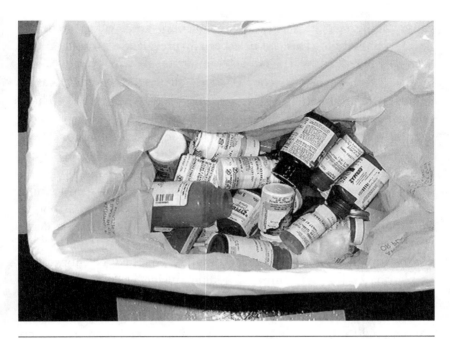

Figure 10.1   In this case of a double suicide, the wife dumped both her and her husband's pills into one pile and they ingested the medications. After that, she made certain the bird had food and water. The couple died with their arms around each other.

with drug abuse, familiar negative factors including physical and sexual abuse and low self-esteem also place an adolescent at high risk for suicide. The use of illicit drugs accompanied by school experience of rejection and/or bullying deserves attention and further study.

Acetaminophen is another drug often found. An overdose can cause death within 24 hours. Even aspirin can cause death. What we are finding, however, is that oxycodone hydrochloride, or Oxycontin, which is typically prescribed for moderate to severe pain, appears to be the real drug of choice at suicide scenes in many parts of the country. Many people "doctor shop" for prescriptions; in other words, they go to multiple physicians to get prescriptions for the drug and then use that large quantity of pills to commit suicide.

Many people use both drugs and alcohol. When at the scene, the coroner must realize that the presence of alcohol or drugs is not the cause of the suicide; the drugs and alcohol are facilitators to the decision to end life. This can be especially prevalent with some drugs, such as alprazolam or Xanax. To commit suicide with Xanax only is difficult, but when it is coupled with alcohol, it is much easier. Amitriptyline, commonly known as Elavil, is especially deadly. Thirty pills can cause death. To make the situation more difficult, this drug can dissipate within the system, and if the body is not found for several days, the level of fatal toxicity can be very difficult, if not impossible, to determine.

In viewing Tables 10.3 and 10.4, it is important to keep in mind that people are all different. For example, if a person is an alcoholic, the amount of medication or other substances needed to cause death may be drastically reduced.

The Food and Drug Administration has requested the cooperation of pharmaceutical companies in adding suicide warnings to certain antidepressant labels. Interestingly, Elias (2004) reported that although this seems like a good idea on the surface, some medical professionals are opposed to the idea because the warnings would serve as a deterrent to people who need the drugs.

Alcohol and Suicide

In the research we have done on local suicide cases, we have discovered that alcohol is part of many of the cases. According to Dr. William Ralston, Assistant Medical Examiner for the Commonwealth of Kentucky, alcohol by itself rarely causes death (William Ralston, personal interview, March 2, 2004). Certainly, one may consume an inordinate amount of alcohol, and in some cases enough to cause death, but other factors to consider are the individual's drinking habits and the potency of the alcohol itself.

What appears to be more important is the role that alcohol plays in the successful completion of a suicide. A person might consume enough alcohol to lower his or her inhibitions about committing suicide. So, although the investigator might find many containers of consumed alcohol at the suicide scene, the alcohol itself is rarely the cause of death.

Table 10.3   Minimal Lethal Doses of Common Prescription Medications

Name of Prescription	Estimated Minimum Number of Units for Lethal Ingestion by a 150-lb Person
Aspirin	90/5 grains
Benadryl	30/50 mg
Codeine	8/60 mg
Compoz	53/25 mg
Contac	35/capsules
Coricidin	84/tablets
Dalmane	110/30 mg
Darvocet	46/50 mg
Darvon	36/65 ng
Demerol	19/50 mg
Dilantin	66/100 mg
Dristin tablets	78/tablets
Dristin capsules	19/capsules
Excedrin	22/tablets
Librium (Chlordiasepoxide)	330/10 mg
Librium Carbonate	45/35 mg
Luminal	45/30 mg
Methadone	19/5 mg
Nemutal	10/100 mg
Nodoz	120/tablets
Oxycontin	107/25 mg
Percodan	94/4.5 mg
Phenobarbital	47/30 mg
Quaalude	44/150 mg
Ritalin	9/20 mg
Sominex	105/25 mg
Sudafed	31/30 mg
Thorazine	19/50 mg
Tylenol	40/325 mg
Valium	658/5 mg
Xanax	7,500/1 mg

Source: Kentucky State Medical Examiner's Office, Louisville.

Beer appears to be more prevalent in youthful suicide for many reasons, one of which is that it is more readily available than hard liquor. For many youth, alcohol is almost a rite of passage. Alcohol becomes

Table 10.4   List of Toxic Household Products Ingested and Minimal
Doses That May Produce Death

Product	Amount
Bleach	1–6 ounces
Ink	15 ounces
Furniture polish (kerosene)	1 ounce
Iodine	3 ounces
Lighter fluid	1 ounce
Nail polish	1 ounce
Nail polish remover	1 ounce
Paint thinner	3–4 ounces
Shaving lotion	20 ounces

Source: Kentucky State Medical Examiner's Office, Louisville.

part of their daily activities, and the weekends are considered "party time." In many communities, it is fairly easy for a youth to obtain alcohol because it is already present in many homes.

In 2003, a 17-year-old boy was drinking beer with his three friends. They had gotten the beer from the host's home. One of the boys suggested that they play Russian roulette with a twist—instead of each person pointing and firing a gun at his own head, everyone would take a turn firing the gun at another. Tragedy struck when on the third pull, one of the boys was struck and killed. Suicide by proxy? We believe so in this case. However, the coroner's office officially ruled the death a homicide, and the police arrested all three remaining youths. They were transferred to a grand jury and tried as adults. The three are now in a medium security prison serving multiyear sentences (Jefferson County Coroner files).

Conclusion

There is no doubt that depression, alcohol, and drugs are important indicators of a suicidal personality. The alert investigator and the professional researcher should be aware of these factors when they are present in any death scene, especially in a suicide scenario.

What should a therapist look for in a person who is contemplating suicide? Obvious signs in a counseling or therapy session can alert the therapist that suicidal problems are present. When depression becomes an overwhelming concern for the patient or client, the therapist should be aware of the possibility of a suicidal act. If the person says he or she is considering suicide or begins to give away his or her personal possessions, that person needs immediate help. Depression aside, alcoholism and drug abuse are two other indicators of a possible suicidal act.

Although the death investigator might see pills or liquor and beer containers at the death scene, all physical evidence must be considered before ruling that a death was a suicide. It is a monumental task, and one that must be taken seriously and professionally.

11

Suicide and the Future

Suicide has been with us since recorded history. Regardless of the society or the time, the culture or the religion, suicide has been proscribed, and only in certain circumstances has it been condoned.

What does the future hold for mankind and suicide? What are some findings regarding the reasons, impulses, and treatments available for those who are contemplating suicide? What can we learn about the suicidal personality and the death scene that might aid us in the prevention of suicide?

What We Have Learned

The most important fact we have learned about suicide is that there is no one reason for someone to commit suicide. People have numerous reasons—failing health, loss of finances, the death of a life partner, and so on.

We have learned about the main risk factors involved in suicide investigation, and also recognition of the suicidal personality and treatment. These risk factors involve a range of issues such as environmental factors, social factors, biological conditions, and certain psychosocial themes. Consider some of the following concerns.

History of Trauma and Abuse

Research has shown that children who have been abused have higher rates of suicide than do children who have not been abused. For example, Vermeiren, Ruchkin, Leckman, Deboutte, and Schwab-Stone

(2002) reported that children who experience violence in the home as well as in other social institutions are at a higher risk of committing suicide than are other children. This same finding was reported by Kidd and Kral (2002) in their study of adolescents in a outreach center. Their findings indicated that as many as three out of four children reported a history of attempted suicide. In their study, it was not only physical violence that was a predominant factor; drug abuse and intimate relationship dissolutions were also present.

Mental Disorders

There is no doubt that mental disorders play a huge part in the decision to commit suicide. For example, Brent et al. (1999) reported that their study of 140 suicide victims showed that mood disorders, psychopathology, and other psychological problems had quite an impact on the victims. Additionally, depression is a major factor in the decision to commit suicide. Depression has many causes and occurs sometimes as a side effect of medication. Conwell and Brent (1995) reported that depression is one of the most common conditions associated with suicide in older adults. Depression becomes more of a contributing factor when it occurs later in life and may be associated with changes in the brain itself (Merikangas et al., 1994).

In the case of severe mental illness that requires hospitalization, Appleby, Dennehy, Thomas, Faragher, and Lewis (1999) reported that people who had recently been hospitalized and then committed suicide had experienced a reduction in medications and personal mental and physical health care. This occurs despite studies that show that some antipsychotic medications may decrease the incidence of suicide among individuals with severe psychiatric disorders (Muller-Oerlinghausen, 2001; Tondo, Baldessarini, & Hennen, 1999).

People who have a severe mental illness commit suicide at an extremely high rate (Angst, Stassen, & Clayton, 2002). This has important ramifications for those who have been diagnosed with an illness so severe that it requires medication and, in more severe cases, hospitalization. As Lewinsohn et al. (2000) reported people who have a history of depression and mental illness are at high risk for *repeated* attempts at suicide, a finding reinforced by the research of Weissman et al. (1999).

Box 11.1   Symptoms of Depression

Physical

- Aches, pains, or other physical complaints
- Marked changes in appetite
- Change in sleep patterns
- Fatigue

Emotional

- Pervasive sadness
- Apathy
- Decreased pleasure
- Crying for no apparent reason
- Indifference to others

Changes in Thoughts and Feelings

- Feelings of hopelessness and helplessness
- Feelings of worthlessness
- Impaired concentration
- Problems with memory
- Indecisiveness
- Recurrent thoughts of death and suicide

Changes in Behavior

- Loss of interest in previously enjoyed activities
- Neglect of personal appearance
- Withdrawal from people
- Increased use of alcohol
- Increased agitation
- Talking about the "end"

Source: Adapted from Schmall, Lawson, and Stiehl (1990).

Previous Suicide Attempts

Perhaps there is no greater risk factor for a successful suicide attempt than a previous suicide attempt. We have noted this in several cases in our work on the suicide cases in the coroner's office in Louisville. One suicide note stated, "This is my fourth time. I hope this time I get it right." Perhaps previous attempts were unsuccessful because the

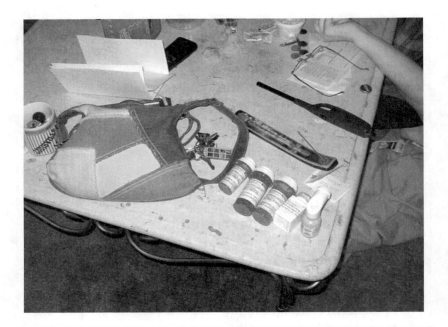

Figure 11.1   This 36-year-old man had tried to kill himself several times
before. He was severely depressed and had been under
medical care for the past several years.

attempts were not sincere. The final, successful attempt might have
built on previous attempts, and the person learned after each try what
would increase the chances for success (see Figure 11.1).

Kempton and Forehand (1992) reported that among youthful
offenders in their study, the majority had attempted suicide at least
once. This was particularly true among white offenders but did not
hold true for black offenders. Adams et al. (1996) found that major
and continuing environmental stressors were common to those who
attempted suicide more than once. These stressors included depression,
low self-worth, drug abuse, and loneliness (Groholt, Ekeberg,
Wichstrom, & Haldorsen, 2000).

Alcohol and Substance Abuse

The use and abuse of alcohol and drugs is a risk factor in suicide
among the young. For example, SAMHSA (2002) reported that in 2000,

more than 3 million young people were at risk of committing suicide. Those especially at risk were youth who abused drugs and alcohol. Sanislow, Grilo, Fehon, Axelrod, and McGlashan (2003) noted in their study that drug abuse, including alcohol, played a significant role for youth who commit suicide. Spirito et al. (2003) said that when one studies the abuse of alcohol among adolescents, and how it may be related to feelings of hopelessness and behavioral problems, it must be considered a serious indicator of suicidal ideation and suicide attempts. Additionally, it plays a significant role in the rehabilitative effort.

Among adults in general, Murphy (2004) found that those who are addicted to drugs or alcohol have a history of abuse that contributes to their suicide. Other studies have found that a history of drug or alcohol abuse plays an integral role regardless of the age cohort studied (Kausch & McCormick, 2002; Murphy, 2002; National Institute on Alcohol Abuse and Alcoholism, 2002).

Financial Losses

As we mentioned in the chapter dealing with the various types of suicide, financial losses sometimes result in a sense of anomie. This feeling of helplessness can create the belief that life no longer has meaning, and that the only way to find peace or completeness is to commit suicide.

Box 11.2   Depression, Alcohol, and Suicide

A direct relationship exists between depression and suicide, alcoholism and depression, and alcoholism and suicide. Studies indicate that the risk of suicide in alcoholics is 50% to 70% greater than in the general population. Studies also show that individuals suffering from a major affective disorder have a suicide rate that is more than 50% higher than that in the general population. Lifetime risk for suicide in the general population is 1%, compared with 15% for persons suffering from depression and 15% for alcoholics. Studies of alcoholics reveal that between 30% and 60% suffer from depression, and a significant proportion of alcoholics have other people in their families suffering from depression.

Source: The Institute on Aging, August 10, 2004. Available: http://www.nia.nih.gov/

Personal or Relationship Losses

Sometimes, the death of a lifelong partner, a parent, or another loved one can result in a sense of dread in facing daily struggles, and a person commits suicide rather than coping with the situation. In cases where the loss is due to divorce, separation, or the breakup of a dating relationship, a person might kill his or her former partner before committing suicide. In other cases, the loss may result in suicide only.

Bolognini et al. (2003) discovered in their study that poor relationships within a family setting are one of the three main reasons for youth's committing suicide. Removal of the familial support system has critical negative effects on a youth's psyche and may result not only in suicidal ideations but also in suicide.

Health Issues

In Chapter 3, in the section on fatalistic suicide, we discussed that some people, when faced with an incurable illness, such as cancer, may decide that the only real way to alleviate the pain and the inevitable is to commit suicide.

Religious Beliefs

We have discussed the mass suicides in the Jonestown and Heaven's Gate communities, and what was apparent in each situation was a religious, spiritual, or dogmatic theme or belief system that almost demanded such action.

Difficulty in Work or Occupational Settings

In the workplace, certain signs may alert coworkers to the possibility that one of their own may be considering suicide. For example, a person might once have been interested in moving up in the organizational structure, but now voices no interest in promotions. A person who was once very neat and organized is now untidy and disorganized. Even giving away personal possessions can be an early sign of contemplating suicide. Or perhaps the person used to work with little or no supervision, but now his or her work product is unclear or incomplete. An alert supervisor can pick up on these clues and try to create a viable plan at work to help the person.

Verbal Hints

In many cases, a person intent on committing suicide will leave verbal hints about what he or she is planning to do. He or she will say such things as "This is my last Christmas" or "I won't be around much longer." The person may even call a loved one, saying, "You won't see me anymore."

Loss of Pleasure in Previously Pleasurable Activities

In many cases, we have seen that once pleasurable activities, such as hobbies or sporting events or activities, now have no special significance for a person. He or she no longer cares about the activity and cannot even pretend to be interested.

Neglect of Personal Appearance

Many individuals with a suicidal ideation will neglect their personal appearance because they no longer care about it. After all, there is no need to attend to personal hygiene if death is only a short time away.

Change in Eating or Sleeping Habits

In the case of someone who is seriously considering suicide, past personal rituals are no longer important. Eating favorite foods, going to restaurants, and so on become less important. Additionally, sleeping habits change drastically. For some people, sleep becomes almost continual, whereas with others, it becomes almost impossible. The important consideration here is that what was once a normal habit has now become abnormal or at least not as important.

Persistent State of Boredom

Many people with suicidal ideation exist in a state of boredom. This boredom may arise in part because of the general anomie that many of them feel. The present state of existence is not important and holds no personal challenges or tasks to accomplish. Life appears to be of no real consequence and to have no real purpose.

Placing Personal Items in Order

An elderly woman who lived alone in her mobile home shot herself in her forehead while lying in bed (see Figure 11.2). When investigating the death scene, the deputy coroner and the coroner noted that on her countertop, she had placed her insurance papers and other

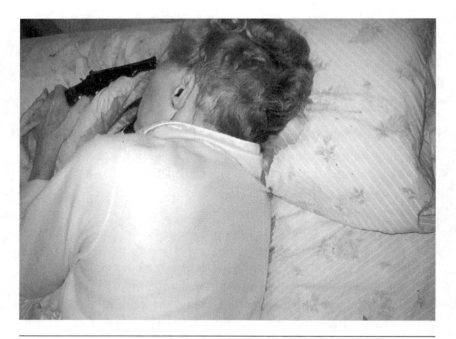

Figure 11.2   The woman left a note explaining her reasons for taking her own life. On the kitchen countertop, she had neatly arranged her life insurance policies, bank information, next-of-kin references, and other pertinent information.

pertinent personal information, including telephone numbers to call to notify her relatives of her death and her own funeral arrangements. She had a prepaid funeral package. The victim had suffered severe health problems, including cancer, diabetes, and an impending operation for back problems. There was a good chance she would be confined to her bed for the remainder of her life. Perhaps in her mind, she was relieving her relatives of any responsibility for her.

Giving Away Personal Possessions

Many people considering suicide make a conscious decision to give away personal and sometimes prized possessions. In one case, a young man gave his fishing poles and bait boxes to his brother a week before he took his own life. The brother mistook the reason for the gifts, thinking his brother was just being generous.

Withdrawal From Primary Group Members

The person contemplating suicide often becomes reclusive. He or she withdraws from communication and association with family and friends, typically because he or she is preparing to commit suicide and is trying to build psychological defenses that will make the suicide easier.

How to Get Better

A number of avenues exist that can help a suicidal individual overcome his or her problems.

- **Medication**—Many medications can help an individual combat the feelings of depression that are common to those who are contemplating suicide. Some medications take longer to be effective than others, and the individual must be aware of this possibility.

- **Support Groups**—Support groups exist for people who have thought of suicide or have survived a suicide attempt. They should be made aware of these groups and make every effort to attend group meetings.

In recent years, schools have begun programs that deal with youth and suicide. These programs often invite community and mental health groups to appear before the students in educational sessions. But as Carr-Gregg (2003) has pointed out, these groups need to be monitored because of some inaccuracies in their information. For example, he reported in his study that some groups actively foster inaccuracies or even distort the truth about suicide. Thus, school administrators and other responsible parties must take an active role in not only the selection of community and mental health groups but also the evaluation of the material and information offered to students. The best programs respond to young people in a helpful and nonjudgmental way and have curricula that contribute to a better understanding of suicide and its causes.

• **Family Therapy**—The suicidal person's entire family would find therapy beneficial because family members can learn techniques to help their loved one. This may be especially true if their loved one is a depressive personality type. Although family therapy does not have all of the answers, it may help the family understand what their loved one is thinking and feeling.

• **Cognitive Therapy**—In conjunction with medication, cognitive therapy—in which a person focuses on his or her problems and also joins in conversation with others who are feeling the same or similar pains—may prove to be very beneficial.

• **Sobriety**—The reduction or elimination of alcohol and drugs from a person's system, as well as an improvement in the person's symptoms of depression, may not be enough on their own, but in conjunction with some of the aforementioned items, these steps can reduce the possibility of suicide.

• **Exercise**—A regimen of physical exercise may keep the body in a healthy state so that thoughts of suicide are less likely.

Thus, what is more beneficial is the combination of two or more of the elements listed above. With the new drugs available and better and faster therapies, treatment has more possibilities for success (Song, 2003).

Organizations for Help

Many local and national organizations can help those who are thinking of committing suicide. Many of the organizations are listed in the local telephone books, but others have Internet pages that are easily accessible.

For example, one organization, called "1 800 SUICIDE," can be reached via the Internet (http://www.hopeline.com/) or simply by dialing 1-800-SUICIDE. Dialing this number automatically routes the call to the crisis center nearest the caller's location. The negative side to this is that the counselor could be several states away.

Another Internet site is SuicideHotlines.com (http://suicidehotlines.com), which can be accessed in seconds. The viewer is directed to select a particular state, and then all of the organizations for that state are listed by city. There are also directions in cases of emergency as well as other telephone numbers that may assist the person.

On the other hand, national organizations exist that provide an educational message. For example, the National Strategy for Suicide Prevention (NSSP) has several links on its Web site to suicide facts, suicide around the world, frequently asked questions about suicide, policies and legislation regarding suicide, and other links. This Web site can be found at http://www.mentalhealth.samhsa.gov/suicideprevention/.

Probably one of the more visible Web sites for the understanding and prevention of suicide is the American Association of Suicidology (AAS) (http://www.suicidology.org). This organization provides education and resources about suicide rather than direct help. It sponsors conferences, has timely publications, and offers both a directory of suicide prevention and crisis intervention agencies in the United States and a directory of survivor support groups.

Another Web site, http://www.groww.org, is a grief support organization that has many chat rooms, one of which is for those who have lost a loved one to suicide. The Suicide Awareness Voices of Education, the Suicide Prevention Advocacy Network, the Samaritans, and the Yellow Ribbon Program are all programs and organizations that want to alleviate the social problem of suicide as well as provide services for survivors.

Other organizations deal specifically with suicide and drugs. In examining some of the Web sites, two sites stand out in terms of helping a particular kind of drug addiction and client base. One is "Hope by the Sea" (http://www.hopebythesea.com), a program that caters to both men and women with drug dependency problems that could result in suicidal ideation. The other is "Stepping Ahead" (http://www.halfwayhouse.net), which caters to women only who have drug and/or alcohol problems.

We would encourage anyone with a personal concern to contact reputable organizations. Counselors and therapists can provide recommendations.

Conclusion

In this chapter, we have examined the suicide problem from various perspectives. For example, we have briefly reexamined a history of abuse, mental disorders, previous suicide attempts, and other concerns. Then, we moved on to microlevel concerns, such as the person giving away prized possessions or giving verbal hints about suicidal intentions.

We then discussed organizations that can provide assistance to suicidal individuals and their families. We believe that such organizations are legitimate and operate with a manifest goal of service to those in need. They offer information, hope, and encouragement.

As stated previously, suicide is a complex behavior. DeAngelis (2001) says that we may never know *the* reason a person commits suicide. This is a multifaceted problem with a serious consequence, and social isolation, lack of personal or intimate relationships, depression, and/or a lack of adequate coping skills may all play some role in a person's decision to commit suicide. The death investigator must be aware of the gravity of the social problem of suicide, help to investigate a potential suicide death scene, know how to arrive at a determination of suicide, and then make proper and humane notification to the next of kin. This is an important role in the work of the death investigator, perhaps the most important role.

References

Achté, K. (1988). Suicidal tendencies in the elderly. *Suicide and Life-Threatening Behavior, 18*(1), 55–65.

Adams, D., Overholser, J., & Spirito, A. (1996). Suicide attempts and stressful life events. *Prevention Researcher, 3*(3), 5–8.

Alexopoulos, G. (2000). Mood disorders. In B. J. Sadock & V. A. Sadock (Eds.), *Comprehensive textbook of psychiatry* (7th ed.). Baltimore: Williams and Wilkins.

Alexopoulos, G., Bruce, M., Hull, J., Sirey, J., & Kakuma, T. (1999). Clinical determinations of suicidal ideation and behavior in geriatric depression. *Annals of General Psychiatry, 56*(11), 1048–1053.

Americans United for Life. (2001). *Physician-assisted suicide: Legislation and policy guide.* Available: http://www.unitedforlife.org/guides/pas/pas.htm

Angst, F., Stassen, H., & Clayton, P. (2002). Mortality of patients with mood disorders: Follow-up over 34–38 years. *Journal of Affective Disorders, 68,* 167–181.

Appleby, L., Dennehy, J. A., Thomas, C. S., Faragher, E. B., & Lewis, G. (1999). Aftercare and clinical characteristics of people with mental illness who commit suicide: A case-control study. *Lancet, 353,* 1397–1400.

Bascom, P., & Tolle, S. (2002). Responding to requests for physician-assisted suicide. *Journal of the American Medical Association, 288*(1), 91–98.

Baumeister, R. (1990). Suicide as escape from self. *Psychological Review, 97*(1), 90–113.

Bearman, P. S. (1992). Issues and alternatives in comparative social research. In C. Ragin (Ed.), *Contemporary sociology.* New York: Wadsworth.

Beyer, M. (1998). Mental health care for children in corrections. *Children's Legal Rights Journal, 8*(3), 18–35.

Blank, K., Robison, J., Doherty, E., Prigerson, H., Duffy, J., & Schwartz, H. I. (2001). Life-sustaining treatment and assisted death choices in depressed older patients. *Journal of the American Geriatrics Society, 49*(2), 153–161.

Bolognini, M., Plancherel, B., Laget, J., & Halfon, O. (2003). Adolescents' suicide attempts: Populations at risk, vulnerability, and substance use. *Substance Use and Misuse, 38,* 1651–1669.

Borrill, J., Burnett, R., Atkins, R., Miller, S., Briggs, D., Weaver, T., & Maden, A. (2003). Patterns of self-harm and attempted suicide among white and black/mixed race female prisoners. *Criminal Behavior and Mental Health, 13*(4), 229–240.

Breed, W. (1963). Occupational mobility and suicide among white males. *American Sociological Review, 28,* 179–188.

Brent, D., Baugher, M., Bridge, J., Chen, T., & Chiappetta, L. (1999). Age and sex-related risk factors for adolescent suicide. *Journal of the American Academy of Child and Adolescent Psychiatry, 38*(12), 1497–1505.

Brown, G., Beck, A., Steer, R., & Grisham, J. (2000). Risk factors for suicide in psychiatric outpatients: A 20-year prospective study. *Journal of Clinical Psychology, 68*(3), 371–377.

Bruce, M., Ten Have, T., Reynolds, C. F. III, Katz, I., Schulberg, H. C., Mulsant, B., Brown, G., McAvay, G., Pearson, J., & Alexopoulos, G. (2004). Reducing suicidal ideation and depressive symptoms in depressed older primary care patients: A randomized controlled trial. *Journal of the American Medical Association, 291*(9), 1081–1091.

Caplan, A., Snyder, L., & Faber-Langendoen, K. (2000). The role of guidelines in the practice of physician-assisted suicide. *Annals of Internal Medicine, 132,* 476–481.

Carr-Gregg, M. (2003). Suicide, schools and young people: Tackling the youth suicide industry. *Youth Studies Australia, 22*(3), 32–35.

Centers for Disease Control and Prevention. (2003). Available: http://www.cdc.gov/nchs/about/major/dvs/mortdata.htm

Chin, A., Hedberg, K., Higginson, G., & Fleming, D. (1999). Legalized physician-assisted suicide in Oregon—The first year's experience. *New England Journal of Medicine, 340,* 577–583.

Clark, D. (1993). Narcissistic crises of aging and suicidal despair. *Suicide and Life-Threatening Behavior, 23*(1), 21–26.

Cohen, D. (2004). *Homicide/suicide in older persons: How you can help prevent a tragedy.* Available: http://www.fmhi.usf.edu/amh/homicide-suicide/art_hs_inolder.html

Comstock, G., & Tonascia, J. (1978). Education and mortality in Washington County, Maryland. *Journal of Health and Social Behavior, 18,* 54–61.

Conaghan, S., & Davidson, K. (2002). Hopelessness and the anticipation of positive and negative future experiences in older parasuicidal adults. *British Journal of Clinical Psychology, 41*(3), 233–242.

Conner, K., Cerulli, C., & Caine, E. (2002). Threatened and attempted suicide by partner-violent male respondents petitioned to family violence court. *Violence and Victims, 17*(2), 115–125.

Conner, K., Duberstein, P., Conwell, Y., and Caine, E. (2003). Reactive aggression and suicide: Theory and evidence. *Aggression and Violent Behavior, 8*(4), 413–432.

Conwell, Y., & Brent, D. (1995). Suicide and aging: Patterns of psychiatric diagnosis. *International Psychogeriatrics, 7*(2), 149–164.

Conwell, Y., Duberstein, P., & Caine, E. (2002). Risk factors for suicide in later life. *Biological Psychiatry, 52*(3), 193–204.

Daigle, M., Alarie, M., & Lefebvre, P. (1999). Problem of suicide among female prisoners. *Forum on Corrections Research, 11*(3), 41–45.

DeAngelis, T. (2001). Unraveling the mystery of suicide: Questions remain on what motivates people to take their own lives. *Monitor on Psychology, 32*(10), 1–3.

Doerflinger, R. (1999). An uncertain future for assisted suicide. *Hastings Center Report, 29,* 52.

Downey, A. (1991). The impact of drug abuse upon adolescent suicide. *Omega, 22*(4), 261–275.

Draper, B., MacCuspie-Moore, C., & Brodaty, H. (1998). Suicidal ideation and the "wish to die" in dementia patients: The role of depression. *Age and Ageing, 27*(4), 503–507.

Durkheim, E. (1951). *Suicide: A study in sociology* (J. A. Spaulding & G. Simpson, Trans.). New York: Free Press.

Elias, M. (2004, October 18). Antidepressant debate takes a delicate turn. *USA Today.* Available: http://www.usatoday.com/news/health/2004-10-18-antidepressant-usat_x.htm

Faber-Langendoen, K., & Karlawish, J. (2000). Should assisted suicide be only physician assisted? *Annals of Internal Medicine, 132*(6), 482–487.

Farganis, J. (Ed.). (2000). *Readings in social theory: The classic tradition to post-modernism* (3rd ed.). Boston: McGraw-Hill.

Federal Bureau of Investigation. (various years). *Supplementary homicide reports, 1976-2000.* Washington, DC: U.S. Government Printing Office.

Fletcher, M., Tortolero, S., Baumer, E., Vernon, S., & Weller, N. (2002). Lifetime inhalant use among alternative high school students in Texas: Prevalence and characteristics of users. *American Journal of Drug and Alcohol Abuse, 28*(3), 477–495.

Florida, R. (1993). Buddhist approaches to euthanasia. *Studies in Religion/ Sciences Religieuses, 22,* 35–47.

Foxhall, K. (2001). Suicide by profession: Lots of confusion, inconclusive data. *Monitor on Psychology, 32*(1), 1–2.

Fyfe, W. (1997). *The histories.* New York: Oxford University Press.

Gallup Poll. (1999, March 12-14). Available: www.pollingreport.com

Geberth, V. (1996). *Practical homicide investigation* (3rd ed.). New York: CRC.

Gesensway, D. (1995, January). Assisted suicide: It's the law in Oregon, but is it ethical? *ACP Observer.*

Gibbs, J., & Porterfield, A. (1960). Occupational prestige and social mobility of suicides in New Zealand. *American Journal of Sociology, 66,* 147–152.

Goldstein, M., & Goldstein, H. (1992). *Dealing with childhood depression and teen suicide.* Plainview, NY: Bureau for At-Risk Youth.

Goodwin, F., Fireman, B., Simon, G., Hunkeler, E., Lee, J., & Revicki, D. (2003). Suicide risk in bipolar disorder during treatment with lithium and divalproex. *Journal of the American Medical Association, 290*(11), 1467–1473.

Gould, M., Greenberg, T., Velting, D., & Shaffer, D. (2003). Youth suicide risk and preventive interventions: A review of the past 10 years. *Journal of the American Academy of Child and Adolescent Psychiatry, 42*(4), 386–405.

Graves, R. (1996). *The annals of imperial Rome.* New York: Penguin.

Greene, J. M., & Ringwalt, C. L. (1996). Youth and familial substance use's association with suicide attempts among runaway and homeless youth. *Substance Use and Misuse, 31*(8), 1041–1058.

Groholt, B., Ekeberg, O., Wichstrom, L., & Haldorsen, T. (2000). Young suicide attempters: A comparison between a clinical and an epidemiological sample. *Journal of the American Academy of Child and Adolescent Psychiatry, 39*(7), 868–875.

Hackett, D. (2003). Suicide and the police. In D. Hackett & J. Violanti (Eds.), *Police suicide: Tactics for prevention* (pp. 7–15). Springfield, IL: Charles C Thomas.

Hayes, L. (2000). Suicide prevention in juvenile facilities. *Juvenile Justice, 7*(1), 24–32.

Heim, C., Newport, D. J., Heit, S., Graham, Y., Wilcox, M., Bonsall, R., Miller, A., & Nemeroff, C. (2000). Pituitary-adrenal and autonomic responses to stress in women after sexual and physical abuse in childhood. *Journal of the American Medical Association, 284*(5), 592–597.

Heisel, M. (2004). Suicide ideation in the elderly. *Psychiatric Times, 21*(3), 1–11.

Henry, A., & Short, J. (1954). *Suicide and homicide: Some economic, sociological, and psychological aspects of aggression.* Glencoe, IL: Free Press.

Hoffman, B., & McCormick, G. (2004). Terrorism, signaling, and suicide attack. *Studies in Conflict and Terrorism, 27,* 243–281.

Holmes, R., & Holmes, S. (2001). *Mass murder in the United States.* Upper Saddle River, NJ: Prentice Hall.

Holmes, R., & Holmes, S. (2004). *Suicide in Louisville, Kentucky.* Unpublished manuscript.

Hovey, J. (1999). Religion and suicidal ideation in a sample of Latin American immigrants. *Psychological Reports, 85,* 171–177.

Huey, S. J., Jr., Henggeler, S., Rowland, M., Halliday-Boykins, C., Cunningham, P., Pickrel, S., & Edwards, J. (2004). Multisystemic therapy effects on attempted suicide by youths presenting psychiatric emergencies. *Journal of the American Academy of Child and Adolescent Psychiatry, 43*(2), 183–190.

Jick, H., Kaye, J., & Jick, S. (2004). Antidepressants and the risk of suicidal behaviors. *Journal of the American Medical Association, 292*(3), 338–343.

Joiner, T. E., Jr., Rudd, M., Rouleau, M., & Wagner, K. (2000). Parameters of suicidal crises vary as a function of previous suicide attempts in youth inpatients. *Journal of the American Academy of Child and Adolescent Psychiatry, 39*(7), 876–880.

Kark, J., Shemi, G., Friedlander, Y., Martin, O., Manor, O., & Blondheim, S. (1996). Does religious observance promote health? Mortality in secular vs. religious kibbutzim in Israel. *American Journal of Public Health, 86,* 341–346.

Kausch, O., & McCormick, R. (2002). Suicide prevalence in chemical dependency programs: Preliminary data from a national sample, and an examination of risk factors. *Journal of Substance Abuse and Treatment, 22*(2), 97–102.

Kempton, T., & Forehand, R. (1992). Suicide attempts among juvenile delinquents: The contribution of mental health factors. *Behavior Research and Therapy, 30*(5), 537–541.

Kidd, S., & Kral, M. (2002). Suicide and prostitution among street youth: A qualitative analysis. *Adolescence, 37*(146), 411–430.

Klerman, G. (Ed.). (1986). *Suicide and depression among adolescents and young adults.* Washington, DC: American Psychiatric Press.

Knowing reasons for suicide in the elderly: First tool for prevention. (2003, April 22). *American Medical Association Science News,* pp. 1–2.

Langevin, R., Paitich, D., Orchard, B., Handy, L., & Russon, A. (1982). The role of alcohol, drugs, suicide attempts and situational strains in homicide committed by offenders seen for psychiatric assessment: A controlled study. *Acta Psychiatrica Scandinavica, 66*(3), 229–242.

Larson, S., & Larson, D. (1990, May/June). Divorce: A hazard to your health? *Physician,* p. 14.

Laws, K., & Turner, A. (1993). *Alcohol and other drug use: The connection to youth suicide: Abstracts of selected research.* Portland, OR: Northwest Regional Educational Laboratory.

Leary, D. (1992). Fast cars don't kill me: Marginalised young people, HIV, and suicide. In S. McKillop (Ed.), *Preventing youth suicide.* Canberra: Australian Institute of Criminology.

Lester, D. (1992). Religiosity, suicide, and homicide: A cross-national examination. *Psychological Reports, 71,* 182.

Lester, D., Yang, B., & Lindsay, M. (2004). Suicide bombers: Are psychological profiles possible? *Studies in Conflict & Terrorism, 27,* 283–295.

Levy, D., Stewart, K., & Wilbur, P. M. (1999, July). *Cost of underage drinking.* Paper presented at the OJJDP National Leadership Conference, Reston, VA.

Lewinsohn, P., Rohde, P., Seeley, J., Klein, D., & Gotlib, I. (2000). Natural course of adolescent major depressive disorder in a community sample: Predictors of recurrence in young adults. *American Journal of Psychiatry, 157,* 1584–1591.

Liska, A. (1987). *Perspectives on deviance.* Englewood Cliffs, NJ: Prentice Hall.

Lloyd, C. (1992). Inmate suicide: What do we know? *Forum on Corrections Research, 4*(3), 5–7.

Loo, R. (2003). Effective postvention for police suicide. In D. Hackett & J. Violanti (Eds.), *Police suicide: Tactics for prevention* (pp. 88–104). Springfield, IL: Charles C Thomas.

Loucks, N. (1998). *HMPI Cornton Vale: Research into drugs and alcohol, violence and bullying, suicides and self-injury and backgrounds of abuse* (Scottish Prison Service Occasional Papers Report No. 1). Edinburgh: Scottish Prison Service.

Ludwig, J., & Cook, P. (2000). Homicide and suicide rates associated with implementation of the Brady Handgun Violence Prevention Act. *Journal of the American Medical Association, 284*(5), 585–591.

Luoma, J., & Pearson, J. (2002). Suicide and marital status in the United States, 1991–1996: Is widowhood a risk factor? *American Journal of Public Health, 92*(9), 1518–1522.

Mahowald, M., Schenck, C., Goldner, M., Bachelder, V., & Cramer-Bornemann, M. (2003). Parasomnia pseudo-suicide. *Journal of Forensic Sciences, 48*(5), 1158-1162.

Maltsberger, J. (1991). The prevention of suicide in adults. In A. Leenaars (Ed.), *Life span perspectives of suicide* (pp. 295-307). New York: Plenum.

Margo, G., & Finkel, J. (1990). Early dementia as a risk factor for suicide. *Hospital and Community Psychiatry, 41*(6), 676–678.

Mastekaasa, A. (1995). Age variations in the suicide rates and self-reported subjective well-being of married and never-married persons. *Journal of Community & Applied Social Psychology, 5*, 21–39.

McEvoy, A., & McElroy, M. (1994). Youth suicide: Comprehensive primary prevention. *School Intervention Report, 7*(3), 1–16.

Merikangas, K., Wicki, W., & Angst, J. (1994). Heterogeneity of depression: Classification of depressive subtypes by longitudinal course. *British Journal of Psychiatry, 164*, 342–348.

Minkoff, K., Bergman, E., Beck, A., & Beck, R. (1973). Hopelessness, depression, and attempted suicide. *American Journal of Psychiatry, 130*(4), 455–459.

Molnar, B. E., Shade, S. B., Kral, A.H., & Watters, J. K. (1998). Suicidal behavior and sexual/physical abuse among street youth. *Child Abuse & Neglect, 22*(3), 213–222.

Morrison, J. L. (1988). Perpetrator suicide following incest reporting: Two case studies. *Child Abuse & Neglect, 12*(1), 115–117.

Muller-Oerlinghausen, B. (2001). Arguments for the specificity of the antisuicidal effect of lithium. *European Archives of Psychiatry and Clinical Neuroscience, 251*(Suppl.), 1172–1175.

Murphy, G. (2002). Alcoholism, drug abuse, and suicide in the elderly. In M. Gurnack, R. Atkinson, & N. Osgood (Eds.), *Treating alcohol and drug abuse in the elderly* (pp. 72-82). New York: Springer.

Murphy, G. (2004). *Suicide in alcoholism.* New York: Oxford University Press.

Narrow, W. E. (2000). *One-year prevalence of depressive disorders among adults 18 and over in the U.S.: NIMH ECA prospective data.* Unpublished table.

National Center for Health Statistics. (2002). *Deaths: Leading causes for 2000.* Available: http://www.cdc.gov/nchs/pressroom/02facts/final2000.htm

National Institute on Alcohol Abuse and Alcoholism. (2002). *Alcohol consumption and problems in the general population. Findings from the 1992 National Longtudinal Alcohol Epidemiologic Survey* (NIH Publication No. 02–4997). Bethesda, MD: Author.

Neeleman, J. (1998). Regional suicide rates in the Netherlands: Does religion still play a role? *International Journal of Epidemiology, 27*, 466–472.

Nelson, F., Farberow, N., & Litman, R. (1988). Youth suicide in California: A comparararive study of perceived causes and interventions. *Community Mental Health Journal, 24*(1), 31–42.

Nepos, C. (1971). *Lives of famous men* (G. Schmeling, Trans.). Lawrence, KS: Coronado.

Office of National Drug Control Policy. (2003). *Cocaine.* Available: http://www
.whitehousedrugpolicy.gov/publications/factsht/cocaine/index.html

Pasewark, R., & Fleer, J. (1993). Suicide in Wyoming, 1960–75. *Journal of
Rural Community Psychology, 12*(2), 39–41.

Patros, P., & Shamoo, T. (1989). *Depression and suicide in children and
adolescents.* Boston: Allyn & Bacon.

Penn, J. V., Esposito, C. L., Schaeffer, L. E., Fritz, G. K., & Spirito, A. (2003).
Suicide attempts and self-mutilative behavior in a juvenile correctional facility. *Journal of American Academy of Child and Adolescent Psychiatry,
42*(6), 762–769.

Peters, D. K., & Range, L. M. (1995). Childhood sexual abuse and current
suicidality in college women and men. *Child Abuse & Neglect, 19*(3),
335–341.

Phillips, D., & Carstensen, L. (1986). Clustering of teenage suicides after television news stories about suicide. *New England Journal of Medicine,
315*(11), 685–689.

Phillips, D., & Paight, D. (1987). The impact of televised movies about suicide.
New England Journal of Medicine, 317(13), 809–811.

Pope, W. (1976). Durkheim's Suicide: *A classic reanalyzed.* Chicago:
University of Chicago Press.

Porsteinsson, A., Duberstein, P., Conwell, Y., Cox, C., Forbes, N., & Caine. E.
(1997). Suicide and alcoholism: Distinguishing alcoholic patients with and
without comorbid drug abuse. *American Journal of Addictions, 6*(4),
304–310.

Radice, B. (Trans.). (1963). *The letters of the Younger Pliny.* Baltimore, MD:
Penguin.

Ragin, D., Pilotti, M., Madry, L., Sage, R. E., Bingham, L. E., & Primm, B. J.
(2002). Intergenerational substance abuse and domestic violence as familial risk factors for lifetime attempted suicide among battered women.
Journal of Interpersonal Violence, 17(10), 1027–1045.

Remafedi, G. (2002). Suicidality in a venue-based sample of young men who
have sex with men. *Journal of Adolescent Health, 31*(4), 305–310.

Rennison, C. (2003). *Intimate partner violence, 1993-2001* (Bureau of Justice
Statistics Crime Data Brief No. NCJ 197838). Washington, DC: Bureau
of Justice Statistics.

Rubio, A., Vestner, A., Wilhelmsson, K., & Alleback, P. (2001). Suicide and
Alzheimer's pathology in the elderly: A case-control study. *Biology and
Psychiatry, 49*(2), 137–145.

Sabatino, D., & Smith, R. (1990). Diagnosis of youth at-risk for suicide, pregnancy, and drug and alcohol abuse. In L. Kruger (Ed.), *Promoting success
with at-risk students: Emerging perspectives and practical approaches*
(pp. 25–41). Binghamton, NY: Haworth.

Sadavoy, J. (1988). Character disorders in the elderly: An overview. In M. Leszcz & J. Sadavoy (Eds.), *Treating the elderly with psychotherapy: The scope for change in later life.* Madison, CT: International Universities Press.

Sanislow, C., Grilo, C., Fehon, D., Axelrod, S., & McGlashan, T. (2003). Correlates of suicide risk in juvenile detainees and adolescent inpatients. *Journal of the American Academy of Child and Adolescent Psychiatry, 42*(2), 234–240.

Schmall, V. L., Lawson, L., & Stiehl, R. (1990). *Depression in later life: Recognition and treatment* (Pacific Northwest Extension Publication PNW 347). Corvallis: Oregon State University Press.

Schneck, S. (1998). "Doctoring" doctors and their families. *Journal of the American Medical Association, 280*(23), 2039–2042.

Serin, R., Motiuk, L., & Wichman, C. (2002). Examination of suicide attempts among inmates. *Forum on Corrections Research, 14*(2), 40–42.

Sheras, P. (2000). *Depression and suicide in juvenile offenders.* Juvenile Justice Fact Sheet. Charlottesville: University of Virginia, Institute of Law, Psychiatry & Public Policy.

Shneidman, E. (1991). Key psychological factors in understanding and managing suicidal risk. *Journal of Geriatric Psychiatry, 24*(2), 153–174.

Siegrist, M. (1966). Church attendance, denomination, and suicide ideology. *Journal of Social Psychology, 136,* 559–566.

Silverman, J., Raj, A., Mucci, L., & Hathaway, J. (2001). Dating violence against adolescent girls and associated substance use, unhealthy weight control, sexual risk behavior, pregnancy, and suicidality. *Journal of the American Medical Association, 286*(5), 572–579.

Simon, R. (1989). Silent suicide in the elderly. *Bulletin of the American Academy of Psychiatry and the Law, 17*(1), 83–95.

Simpson, G. (1963). *Emile Durkheim: Selections from his work.* New York: Crowell.

Skoog, I., Aevarsson, O., Beskow, J., Larsson, L., Palsson, S., Waern, M., Landahl, S., & Ostling, S. (1996). Suicidal feelings in a population sample of nondemented 85-year-olds. *American Journal of Psychiatry, 153,* 1015–1020.

Slatkin, A. (2003). Suicide risk and hostage/barricade situations involving older persons. *FBI Law Enforcement Bulletin, 72*(4), 26–32.

Slome, L., Mitchell, T., Charlebois, E., Benevedes, J., & Abrams, D. (1997). Physician-assisted suicide and patients with human immunodeficiency virus disease. *New England Journal of Medicine, 336*(6), 417–421.

Snyder, L., & Caplan, A. (2000). Assisted suicide: Finding common ground. *Annals of Internal Medicine, 132,* 468–469.

Soloff, P., Lynch, K., Kelly, T., Malone, K., & Mann, J. (2000). Characteristics of suicide attempts of patients with major depressive episode and borderline personality disorder: A comparative study. *American Journal of Psychiatry, 157,* 601–608.

Song, S. (2003, September 22). How to get better. *Time,* p. 49.

Spirito, A., Mehlenbeck, R., Barnett, N., Lewander, W., & Voss, A. (2003). Relation of mood and behavior to alcohol use in adolescent suicide attempters. *Journal of Child & Adolescent Substance Abuse, 12*(4), 35–53.

Stack, S., & Lester, D. (1991). The effect of religion on suicide ideation. *Social Psychiatry and Psychiatric Epidemiology, 26,* 168–170.

Stockard, J., & O'Brien, R. (2002). Cohort variations and changes in age-specific suicide rates over time: Explaining variations in youth suicide. *Social Forces, 81*(2), 605–642.

Straus, M. A., & Kantor, G. K. (1991). *Physical punishment by parents: A risk factor in the epidemiology of depression, suicide, alcohol abuse, child abuse, and wife beating.* Durham, NH: Family Research Lab.

Substance Abuse and Mental Health Services Administration. (2002). *Substance use and the risk of suicide among youths.* Available: http://www.oas.samhsa .gov/2k2/suicide/suicide.htm

Tartaro, C. (2003). Suicide and the jail environment: An evaluation of three types of institutions. *Environment and Behavior, 35*(5), 605–620.

Thompson, E., Franklin, N. D., & Eggert, L. L. (2000). Inhalant use among youth across a decade: 1990-1999. *Prevention Researcher, 7*(3), 7–9.

Thompson, K. (1982). *Emile Durkheim.* London: Tavistock.

Tjaden, P., & Thoennes, N. (2000). *Full report of the prevalence, incidence, and consequences of violence against women: Findings from the National Violence Against Women Survey.* NIJ Research Report. Washington, DC: National Institute of Justice.

Tondo, L., Baldessarini, R. J., & Hennen, J. (1999). Lithium and suicide risk in bipolar disorder. *Primary Psychiatry, 6, 51–56.*

Treisman, G., Angelino, A., & Hutton, H. (2001). Psychiatric issues in the management of patients with HIV infection. *Journal of the American Medical Association, 286*(22), 2857–2864.

Tulsky, J. (2000). Responding to legal requests for physician-assisted suicide. *Annals of Internal Medicine, 132*(6), 494–499.

Vacco v. Quill, 117 S.Ct. 2293 (1997).

Vermeiren, R., Ruchkin, V., Leckman, P., Deboutte, D., & Schwab-Stone, M. (2002). Exposure to violence and suicide risk in adolescents: A community study. *Journal of Abnormal Child Psychology, 30*(5), 529–537.

Vital Statistics of the United States. (2000). *Mortality.* Available: http://www .cdc.gov/nchs/products/pubs/pubd/vsus/vsus.htm

Waern, M., Runeson, B., Allebeck, P., Beskow, J., Rubenowitz, E., Skoog, I., & Wilhelmsson, K. (2002). Mental disorder in elderly suicides: A case-control study. *American Journal of Psychiatry, 159*(3), 450–455.

Wardarski, J., & Harris, P. (1993). Adolescent suicide: A review of the influences and means for prevention. *Social Work, 32*(6), 477–484.

Weissman, M., Wolk, S., Goldstein, R., Moreau, D., Adams, P., Greenwald, S., Klier, C., Ryan, N., Dahl, R., & Wickramaratne, P. (1999). Depressed adolescents grown up. *Journal of American Medical Association, 281,* 1707–1713.

White, H. (1912). *Appian's Roman history: Vol. 3: The civil wars.* New York: Macmillan.

Wild, N. J. (1988). Suicide of perpetrators after disclosure of child sexual abuse. *Child Abuse & Neglect, 12*(1), 119–121.

Yexley, M., Borowsky, I., & Ireland, M. (2002). Correlation between different experiences of intrafamilial physical violence and violent adolescent behavior. *Journal of Interpersonal Violence, 17*(7), 707–720.

Yoder, K. A., Hoyt, D. R., & Whitbeck, L. B. (1998). Suicidal behavior among homeless and runaway adolescents. *Journal of Youth and Adolescence, 27,* 753–771.

Youth Suicide League. (2003). Available: http://www.unicef.org/pon96/insuicid.htm

Zametkin, A., Alter, M., & Yemini, T. (2001). Suicide in teenagers: Assessment, management, and prevention. *Journal of the American Medical Association, 286*(24), 3120–3125.

Zimbardo, P. (1997). What messages are behind today's cults? *APA Monitor, 28*(5), 14.

Zweig, J., Phillips, S., & Lindberg, L. (2002). Predicting adolescent profiles of risk: Looking beyond demographics. *Journal of Adolescent Health, 31*(4), 343–353.

Index

About the Authors

Ronald M. Holmes is Coroner in the Jefferson County Coroner's Office and Professor Emeritus of Justice Administration at the University of Louisville in Louisville, Kentucky. He is the author of several books, among them *Profiling Violent Crimes* (1996), *Sex Crimes* (1991), and *Serial Murder* (1988). He is also the author of more than 50 articles appearing in scholarly publications. He is Vice President of the National Center for the Study of Unresolved Homicides and has completed more than 500 psychological profiles for police departments across the United States. He received his doctorate from Indiana University.

Stephen T. Holmes is Assistant Professor of Criminal Justice at the University of Central Florida. Prior to this position, he was a social science analyst for the National Institute of Justice in Washington, DC. He has authored six books and more than 15 articles dealing with policing, drug testing, probation and parole issues, and violent crime. He received his doctorate from the University of Cincinnati.